FIND THE PEARL OF GREAT PRICE!

Memoirs of a Black Mystic From the Bronx

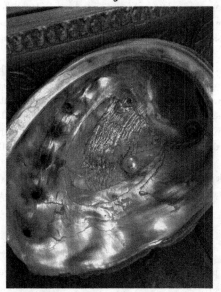

REV. BONITA JONES FRAZIER

BALBOA.PRESS
A DIVISION OF HAY HOUSE

Balboa Press books may be ordered through booksellers or by contacting:

Balboa Press
A Division of Hay House
1663 Liberty Drive
Bloomington, IN 47403
www.balboapress.com
1 (877) 407-4847

Because of the dynamic nature of the Internet, any web addresses or links contained in this book may have changed since publication and may no longer be valid. The views expressed in this work are solely those of the author and do not necessarily reflect the views of the publisher, and the publisher hereby disclaims any responsibility for them.

The author of this book does not dispense medical advice or prescribe the use of any technique as a form of treatment for physical, emotional, or medical problems without the advice of a physician, either directly or indirectly. The intent of the author is only to offer information of a general nature to help you in your quest for emotional and spiritual well-being. In the event you use any of the information in this book for yourself, which is your constitutional right, the author and the publisher assume no responsibility for your actions.

Any people depicted in stock imagery provided by Getty Images are models, and such images are being used for illustrative purposes only.
Certain stock imagery © Getty Images.

Print information available on the last page.

All Scripture quotations are taken from the King James Version.

ISBN: 978-1-9822-4504-7 (sc)
ISBN: 978-1-9822-4506-1 (hc)
ISBN: 978-1-9822-4505-4 (e)

Library of Congress Control Number: 2020905156

Balboa Press rev. date: 03/20/2020

CONTENTS

Acknowledgments.. ix

Foreword xi

Preface xiii

Prologue xv

Chapter 1   The Awakening: The Pearl 1

Chapter 2   Early Childhood 5

Chapter 3   Growing Up..19

Chapter 4   Karma and Reincarnation..........................35

Chapter 5   College 63

Chapter 6   Identity..73

Chapter 7   Finding My Spiritual Community 83

Chapter 8   Encounters with Angels and the Messenger
             Elizabeth Clare Prophet.............................97

Chapter 9   The Dharma.. 105

Chapter 10   To Sum Up 135

Epilogue.. 143

Bibliography 147

To my grandchildren, Isaac Charles, Laila Simone, and Elise Noel.

ACKNOWLEDGMENTS

I would like to express my profound thanks to Shelby Connell, who took time to give me her heartfelt guidance and expertise in editing this work; to my husband Kenneth, for his loving encouragement and probing questions that triggered deeper memories; to Lucy Torres, who worked with me at the beginnings of this project; and to my children, Summer, Michael, and Spirit Ananda, who cheered me on and supported me in this endeavor. I am eternally grateful!

Finally, I would like to give my deepest gratitude and thanks to my teachers, Mark L. and Elizabeth Clare Prophet, and to the ascended masters, for bringing to me the knowledge of "who I am" and what is my purpose for living.

FOREWORD

I was very honored when Bonita asked me to write the foreword to her book about her journey in life. We have been close friends all of our lives, from birth to the present. We were both only children, raised by parents whose close relationship was like family. Though we don't look alike, Bonita could have been my mother's child.

You will find that her book, *Find the Pearl of Great Price! Memoirs of a Black Mystic from the Bronx* will stimulate another level of religious thought. You may not shout halleluiah, but you will look at your life in a different way. This book is a guide that helps you formulate a foundation for religious exploration, and it doesn't make a difference what religion. She doesn't tell you to join this; she says establish a relationship with God. And this is the avenue she explored. Whether you are a philosopher, minister, or layperson, I encourage you to follow the path that this book lays out for you in determining where and when you will find the light we all deserve.

Gail Hawkins Bush,
Former Chair, Mayor's Commission on Women
Alliance for Progress Charter School, Founder and CEO
Harford Community College, Dean of Students

PREFACE

I believe all of us are extraordinary people because we are made in the image of God. The spiritual path I've been following for so many years has revealed to me some of the components of that image. Like a photograph being developed in a dark room, it continues to reveal portions of itself. My being is undergoing a revolution: my thinking, my acting, my feeling are more illumined, more loving more joyful. I knew I had a story to tell and I thought that, in telling mine, it would propel you to search for the meaning of your existence and the mystery of God's image in you.

I started this book project as a self-help book about eight years ago. It has evolved and transformed itself many times as I grew and was transformed myself. I begin with a quite dramatic, true spiritual experience that completely revolutionized my life. This experience, I believe, is for you also. It was the recognition that Christ lives within me—that the answers to all of my desires lie within my own heart. This knowledge brought understanding and illumination about my identity as a God-free being in potential. It answered the questions, Who Am I? And, Why am I here on earth now? Although I am a woman of color and you may be whatever race you are, what happened to me proved to me that my identity is beyond race, culture, and nationality. It is something sublime, perfect, and free. If it is true of me; I believe it is true of you.

Find the Pearl of Great Price! Memoirs of a Black Mystic from the Bronx describes transcendental experiences I've had from the time

I was a child and up to the present moment—experiences that affirm for me what I just told you.

As you read, I suggest you keep a journal to jot down what is meaningful to you. What I share as having happened to me may trigger some memories and experiences of your own that you never gave much thought to at the time, but now you may see them as having special significance. You will want to write them down and think about them.

Although this book's subtitle is _Memoirs of a Black Mystic from the Bronx_, you will note that some of the writing is instructive. Please forgive me this literary departure. I can't help myself. I am a teacher and I like to preach.

I wrote this book for you who are looking for a path that leads all the way home to permanent reunion with God. It is the path of the mystic. May God illumine your heart as your read!

PROLOGUE

MY MESSAGE TO YOU

The Christ is the living Word that Jesus was and is. This living Word is within each of us and needs to be given recognition and loved profoundly. It is what the saints call the divine spark. It is our inner divinity and what I have come to know as the seed of Christ, a living flame[1] within my heart. This presence within me and within you is our birthright and heritage waiting to fully reveal itself in full glory as the universal Christ in all who love God of whatever religion. This presence, the seed of which is the spark within, is the son in the Trinity of Father, Son, and Holy Spirit, and it is universal yet individualized for each one of us. The Hindus speak of it as Vishnu, the Buddhists as the spark within, the Christian mystics as the Hidden Man of the Heart, and there are other names I am sure. This Christ presence is our dearest friend and guardian angel. It is the pearl of great price to be sought, to be experienced, and to become.

I am dedicating these memoirs to you, the light bearer, one who carries the seed of this Christ in your heart, and particularly

---

[1] The threefold flame of power, wisdom, and love represents the three aspects of God as Father, Son, and Holy Spirit and it is the seed of Christ that resides in the spiritual center of our heart called the secret chamber.

For more information on your higher self: Mark L. Prophet and Elizabeth Clare Prophet and staff of Summit University, "Your Higher Self" The *Sacred Adventure Series: The Spiritual Quest* 17, *Meeting the Masters*, 102-111 (Gardiner, Montana: Summit Publications, 2003).

to you who are sons and daughters of Afra,[2] the spiritual shepherds for the black race. Many of us have long forgotten our identity as sons and daughters of God and have wandered far away from this understanding. I am writing to remind you. See, your soul knows, yours and mine, and our souls hunger for reunion with this presence and that conscious oneness that we once shared. The soul is wise because she contains all of the memories of our previous incarnations. How better off we would be if we could benefit from her wisdom! She is not immortal, but she carries within the sphere of her great being the seed of immortality, and she can earn that immortality.

I am going to tell you of my experience of this Christ presence. By sharing my story in these memoirs, you may contemplate what your mission in life is, if you do not already know. You may also start to consider why you were born into the family you are in. What is it that you must learn from your family members and they from you? This knowledge will make you a better son or daughter; a better husband, wife, and friend; a better community member; and a more illumined person. The path of the mystic that I am following is practical, realizable, and often tough. Its rewards are no less than God realization, God love, and God freedom!

A mystic is one who has sought for many lifetimes the direct experience of God, the experience of complete bonding. Jesus the Christ came as the great example of this path of the mystic. The sincere love and obedience Jesus showed the Father and the tender care he gave his fellow man as he walked the earth is

---

[2] Afra, the patron saint of Africa, is an ascended master who graduated from earth's schoolroom five hundred thousand years ago and is the sponsor of the black race and other minorities.

See Elizabeth Clare Prophet, *Afra, Brother of Light* in *Meet the Master Series, Spiritual Teachings from an Ascended Master* (Gardiner, Montana: SU Press, 2003).

something all of us are meant to do in our own way. Sojourner Truth, Rebecca Cox Jackson, Saint Francis of Assisi, Saint Teresa of Avila, Saint John of the Cross, Saint Bakhita of Sudan, and many men and women throughout the ages from all cultures and all religions who loved the divine had this seed of God within them and followed the path of mysticism. *This experience goes by many names, among them the Path of the Kabala in Judaism, the Path of the Sufi in Islam, the Path of the Christian Mystic, the Path of the Bodhisattva in Buddhism, and others.* You too can be a modern-day mystic following your own religious tradition.

The difference between Jesus and us is that Jesus, the Son of Man, was fully integrated with the Christ.[3] He came on a mission to save our souls and to show us how to overcome our sense of human limitation and exchange our concepts of ourselves from poor sinners to sons and daughters of God.

As sons and daughters of God, we are born with a purpose and a mission to fulfill—a divine blueprint to be shepherds to others. My mission is the mission of the mystic that begins with the desire for reunion with the Christ and ultimately with the Mighty I AM Presence,[4] and to preach it and teach it to others who are searching for true liberation. What I share is not a set of exercises, a method to feel more peaceful and centered in order to accommodate life's challenges, although that alone would be of great benefit and may be first steps. I am sharing with you the greatest challenge of all, to become the God-self that you really are. We are God in potential, not God quantitatively but God

---

[3] Elizabeth C Prophet, "Chapter 1: An Experience That Transforms the Soul," in *Becoming God: The Path of the Christian Mystic* (Gardiner, Montana: Summit University Press, 2010.

[4] The "Chart of the Mighty I AM Presence" is a pictorial rendering of our identity in God. Please see figure A. along with its explanation and notes.

qualitatively, like drops of water from the ocean as compared to the ocean. We are composed of the same elements, the same substance—in His image and out of the substance of His being.

I was and am, like you, perfect in design. After many incarnations I find myself today, in this life, Bonita Jones Frazier. My racial designation is black and the black communities of the Bronx, Manhattan, and Long Island where I grew up are the context into which I was born. But being black is not my truest identity, and it does not fully define me. Nor does your race or community fully define you. We may have brown or white skin of various hues now. In other lifetimes, we have worn skin tones of violet, yellow, or red. Today we may be in a female body. In previous lifetimes, we may have been male. For each lifetime, the soul comes outfitted in the perfect garments needed for the lessons she is intended to learn and the service she comes to render.

Find the Pearl of Great Price! Memoirs of a Black Mystic from the Bronx reflects some aspects of the long span of my journey with snippets of events that have occurred over many, many lifetimes. It mostly talks about this life and how a girl from the Bronx found the "pearl of great price," what prompted that search first of all, and what led up to a magnificent spiritual experience that I share with you. It also talks about the influences of my parents, their friends, and my own associations as I matured into a young woman. I make note of some of the trials I have worked through and the joys that have inspired me along the way. This search for "the pearl" has its roots deep in my past. It's not a new adventure for me. Nor is it for you who are on a spiritual path I suspect. It is the picking up of the stitches sewn long ago.

1

The Awakening: The Pearl

It is 1978, in Pasadena, California. I am seated in an auditorium with a group of seekers waiting to hear my first dictation. Dictations are messages from God delivered in these times by an ascended master or cosmic being through their anointed messenger Elizabeth Clare Prophet.[5] I had arrived at the auditorium by myself. I looked around and realized I did not know anyone, yet I was joyous in anticipation of what was about to happen. It was my first conference, "Find Your Way Back to Me," which was an apt title, since I'd been searching since I was twenty-two. During the release of the teachings given at this conference, a divine person filled my being. That person was my best self, the

---

[5] God ordained Elizabeth Clare Prophet and Mark Prophet, her husband, as His messengers. (Guy and Edna Ballard were the ordained messengers in the earlier part of the Twentieth Century through the "I AM" Activity.) The Prophets have given teachings from the ascended hierarch through the aegis of the Holy Spirit recorded in hundreds of books and DVDS. They are the "two olive trees and the two candle sticks" cited in the Book of Revelation, (Rev. 11:4) who would prophesy in these times. The ascended masters, who dictated these teachings, are men and women from every race and culture who fulfilled their reason for being and ascended to the realms of spirit. They are our elder brothers and sisters who through these anointed messengers have brought us the authentic word of progressive revelation.

See Mark L. Prophet and Elizabeth Clare Prophet, "Chapter 4: Messengers", *Foundations of the Path* (Gardiner, Montana: SU Press, 1999), 99.

self that I would come to know as my Holy Christ self. I knew at that moment a peace and comfort I had never experienced in this life. I felt completely whole. God had realigned my understanding, and in this world of relativity, where things have become topsy-turvy and right is left and left right, I knew what was true and who I really was and am—a spark of divinity. My soul rejoiced! In this connectedness to my Christ presence, I could hardly contain myself. I wanted to tell everyone around me; I wanted to shout it out to the world. I affirmed almost out loud, *I must make this a permanent, day-to-day reality!*

I had found the pearl of great price; or better said, Christ had revealed Himself to me as myself, the true nature of my being. This universal presence had always been there, and the fact that I had experienced it so profoundly was a gift. I wanted that integration forever as a conscious daily experience, and I was willing to give all to get it.

This was the powerful catalyst that prompted my search in earnest on this path of reunion with the divine. God often gives us a taste of Himself and our reality and then withdraws while waiting to see how much of it we will pursue. For example, you may have a beautiful flash of intuition. He is showing you what is possible for you to have frequently, but you have to earn it by devotion and good works. As we do pursue this experience with devotion and good works, He allows us to taste more and more. From that hour to the present, it is a presence I feel off and on in both sublime meditation, when I hear a dictation or am praying, and in ordinary, daily routines when I am sensitive and tune in.

I had experienced higher consciousness before in my meditations and practice of yoga but never like this. This was a person! Myself! I thought, *I will follow this path of reunion wherever it leads me.* And it led me to the feet of the ascended masters and their teachings as taught by their anointed messengers, Mark and Elizabeth Clare Prophet.

I am reminded of Jesus's teaching, where in the gospel He says, "Again, the kingdom of heaven is like unto a merchant man, seeking Godly pearls. Who, when he had found one pearl of great price, went and sold all that he had, and bought it" (Matthew 13:45–46 KJV).

Since my early twenties, I had been looking to find the answers to these questions: Who am I? Why am I here on earth? What or who is the divine? And how can I have a conscious perpetual experience with Him/Her?[6] I dabbled in several spiritual disciplines, and none of them held me for very long. So I continued to explore organizations and groups where I might be able to pick up the dropped stitches from previous lifetimes. I don't remember many of my past lives. I get only glimpses, but I see enough to know that this quest has been on a continuum spanning the centuries. Though not aware of the fact then, I sensed I must have been born a mystic, and now I was catching up with what I'd started long ago.

---

[6] "Father is the origin and Mother is the fulfillment of the cycles of God's consciousness expressed throughout the Spirit-Matter creation." You can read more about "The Mother" in Mark L. Prophet and Elizabeth C. Prophet, Saint *Germain on Alchemy: Formulas for Self Transformation* (Gardiner, Montana, SU Press, 1993), glossary.

2

Early Childhood

In this lifetime, I was born in 1942 in New York's Manhattan Hospital. I was a five-pound baby girl and the pride and joy of Edith and Charles Jones. We lived in the Bronx on Trinity Avenue off Boston Road at 166th Street. The neighborhood was racially black and Puerto Rican, and during the hot summer nights folks hung out on the stoops of their apartment buildings to escape the heat. I remember the fishmongers in wagons drawn by horses coming down the street while hawking their fish and the ice slush guy pulling his little wagon of paper cones and blocks of ice. He had various kinds of syrups, and for a few pennies, he'd shave off some ice and make us slush cones. In those days, the latter 1940s, the milkman regularly dropped off bottles of milk with swirls of thick, delicious cream on top. Around the corner and up the street was the local movie theater, with its marquee and billboards featuring John Wayne and Boris Karloff. It looked pretty ordinary on the outside, but once you entered, there were velvet curtains and ornate balconies. One could imagine being in a turn-of-the-century opera house. The admission price was only a quarter. Seems really quaint now. Try getting into a movie for a quarter today!

There was a shoemaker not too far from where I lived, and you could have your shoes fixed or remade there. On Saturdays, my mom picked up our bed sheets from the Chinese laundry, and our whole family slept on fresh, pressed sheets that night.

My block was relatively safe. But some of the kids from the high school nearby were known to extort kids leaving for home. Farther south in the Bronx, there were gangs and rough neighborhoods. Not too far from where we lived was a gang of girls who carried razor blades between their fingers. They would slash people on the subways. I remember everyone in the neighborhood talking about this gang, but I never met anyone who actually saw them or had an encounter with them.

On my block of Trinity Avenue were lots of private homes, three- and four-story apartment buildings, and neighbors who knew each other. Later, the private homes across the street were replaced by projects (low-income housing for welfare recipients). We used to play in the half-empty lots before they were built, running over the planks and two-by-fours that had been torn down but not yet cleared away. The boys on the block made skateboards out of old orange crates. The girls mostly had metal roller skates. We would roller-skate and skateboard in groups all around the neighborhood and beyond till dusk.

Down the street and around the corner was a candy store. It sold big smokes, French fries in small brown bags that quickly turned greasy when full, pickled pigs' feet in jars, Tootsie Rolls, Mounds bars, Almond Joys, newspapers, and a variety of other things. It was also a place where people bet on the daily number— illegal betting before there was the lottery system. There was always a hustle and bustle of activity at this store, with people going and coming, coming and going.

My father, mother, grandmother, and I lived on the second floor of a two-story redbrick home. Annabelle and Pete Richardson, who were our landlords, lived downstairs with their nieces and nephew. They had an old, reddish-brown dog name Joe. One day, quite innocently, I reached out to pet old Joe, and rather than wagging his tail like I thought he would, he bit me.

On the top floor where we lived, there were three bedrooms, a kitchen, family room, and large living room with big windows that looked out on the street. In the back were the bedrooms and one bathroom. A long hallway connected the two areas. Outside, in the back, was a little patch of grass and a parking area. Underneath the apartment was a garage. The floors in our apartment were wooden with fashion rugs spread about. There was an identical house next door—too close next door so no breeze could enter. In the hot summers, the only relief came from the open front windows in the living room or my parents' and grandmother's back bedroom windows. There were no windows in the hallway. It was extremely uncomfortable in the summers, and I had a hard time sleeping at night. In those days, there were no air conditioners, only fans. In the family room was a grand piano, where, on weekends, one could hear my grandmother's chords of Mozart and Rachmaninoff and my father's strands of jazz.

Just up the street from us lived a Catholic family—Evatnie Curtis; her husband; their eight children; and her brother, Lawrence. I went over to their house about once a day, and they always set out a plate of snacks when they saw me coming.

7

Evatnie's mother baked fresh rolls from scratch every Sunday and sent them to our family for Sunday dinner.

My parents were working folk. My father was a lieutenant in the homicide division of the New York Police Department, and my mom was a social worker for Sheltering Arms Children's Service on Twenty-Ninth Street in Manhattan. She helped couples to adopt babies. We were middle-class blacks.

EARLY MYSTICAL EXPERIENCES

One of my first mystical experiences in this life occurred when I was a baby. My mother had left me in the baby carriage in our fenced-in backyard and gone into the house. She was not aware that it had started to rain, and I was getting wet—soaked, as a matter of fact. While my body was being splashed, my soul was immersed in the sound and moisture of the rain. I obviously could not give voice to this experience as a baby. However, as an adult, I remember. It was a snapshot in time and space, a pleasant occasion that quickened within me something very deep. It was the connection to the *now*—oneness with the rain, the drops, and the mist. I had no fear or sense of abandonment.

On another occasion, I was in the kitchen practicing how to tie my shoe. I was fumbling with some brown shoelaces trying to remember how they went—over and under and around then tie. Suddenly, I tied it all by myself! "I did it!" I exclaimed.

It's hard to convey the joy I felt. This accomplishment tapped again into another deeply meaningful awareness; I had no words for it then, but in retrospect, I can say now that I knew at my core I was a powerful being. I was three years old.

We all have had transcendental experiences as children that take us beyond our present awareness into a reality just beyond the ordinary. We put no words to them because, as children, we do not yet have the words. They remain unarticulated until something in our present sparks the memory and we go, Oh wow! That's what it was!

These memories that catapulted from my subconscious into my present awareness were my soul's attempt to communicate the connection between the past, the now, and the future. I think experiences like these are building blocks to our real self and to higher consciousness. Maybe you have not given much thought to them when they have popped up for you. Nevertheless, they leave an impact our inner and outer life that might prompt us to view people and events differently from before that we can't quite explain.

I recall further when I was in Catholic elementary school,

I used to walk the seven blocks to school and home every day. Along the way, I smelled the ragweed and observed the trees and the stray cats and dogs. In the evening, either from my window or while out playing with the neighborhood kids, I saw old black women who looked like grandmas with their gray heads and bent backs. They carried grocery bags and walked slowly home, probably tired after a long day's work. I would see them and think to myself, *oh how I love them.* I saw them as something extraordinary and blessed. Where this feeling came from I do not know. Maybe it was some memory from another life. But at eight years old, I knew these women and could bear witness to their love and sacrifice. From where did that feeling come?

As an only child, I was lonely and had to learn to entertain myself. I read a lot and fantasized a lot. Not having brothers and sisters forced me to become creative for enjoyment. While alone, I lived in my head in a fantasy world, where there were castles and princes on white horses who would come to my rescue. Every night before I fell asleep, I would create a dream where a prince charming would swoop me up and carry me to his castle, and we would live happily ever after. I really got into that stuff.

While this appears to be only a childhood fantasy, in reality, there is more to it. Later in life, I discovered, through my introduction to the teachings of the ascended masters, the story of twin flames carried in the unconscious of humanity. Twin flames are beings that were created from the same blueprint in the beginning when God created us. They are different from soul mates that are two compatible souls that come to serve a similar mission. You can read more about twin flames in Mark L. Prophet and Elizabeth C. Prophet (Twin Flames), Chapter

1: Twin Rays" in *The Path to Attainment* (Gardiner, Montana: SU Press, 2008).

In another aspect of my being I was a tomboy. I loved climbing trees. When I went to visit my cousin Wells in New Jersey on holidays, we climbed trees. And I would get to see my Aunt Lillian, Uncle Rod, and my grandpa Lemuel Evans, who lived with them. My grandfather used to tell the joke that his teeth were like the stars because they came out at night. That would always make me laugh. I have fond memories of Cranford. In the summer, Wells and I went fishing on the Cranford River. And in the winter, when it was frozen, we skated on it. It was kind of funny, tomboy by day and princess by night. I felt comfortable in both roles.

Being an only child also taught me independence and self-reliance. I had to entertain myself, by myself and learn not to be afraid to go places on my own. I also could not lay my faults at the feet of a brother or sister. I had no other sibling to blame when things didn't go well between my parents and me. It also prepared me for the path of mysticism, in that I was alone with myself a lot. The search for union with God is a solitary path—private, personal, and often lonely. Later in life, I welcomed the companionship and support of a loving husband and a spiritual community of souls who were also walking this path.

JANET DALLAS

I had some good friends in those early years from birth to about fourteen. Janet Dallas was one of them. When we were really young, we played having tea with her very fine china tea set.

Another game we played was "shark." The object of this game was to crawl around on the floor in her bedroom until one of us suddenly shouted, "Shark." Then, screaming with glee, we would see who could jump on the bed first to escape the imaginary monster. We had such childlike adventures in her bedroom on 148th street and St Nicolas.

When I was older and in middle school, I used to walk to Janet's from my house in the Bronx. I'd walk down Boston Road to Third Avenue, where trolley cars used to run in the '50s; follow the El (elevated train) down to 155th Street; cross the bridge; and walk down to 148th street. Then I'd turn left on St. Nicholas and head down to the St Nicholas Terrace. I loved to walk and used to do "walking penances" when I thought to correct some misbehavior. This was baked into me from having gone to Catholic school.

Janet and I, as she reminded me when we were adults, were always talking about mission and destiny. We knew there was more to life than having a profession, marrying, and raising children. I do not want to diminish the importance of these experiences. They are very important to our sense of fulfillment and to our obligation to life and the future. Yet, they are backdrops only, dramas of karmic circumstances for our soul's growth and the growth of others who are involved with us on this journey. The associations, friendships, and relatives we have, we need. They provide examples, choices, and opportunities to balance karma as we move toward reunion with the Divine. I believe many of us have had these kinds of thoughts. It was not unique to Janet and me. But for me, our discussions were the watering of the seeds of mysticism, and those seeds were beginning to sprout. Janet later became a minister, as I did.

The game of "shark" particularly reminds me today of what

the ascended masters have taught about the "dweller on the threshold."[7] The dweller is a composite of all of our negative momentums—fears, hatreds, angers, and the like—that we carry in our being lifetime after lifetime. These repressed desires and states of consciousness reside just below the threshold of our conscious awareness, yet their influence is the cause of many of our negative behaviors. The soul alone cannot defeat it because it is too powerful. Like Darth Vader in *Stars Wars*, it has tremendous momentum on the "dark side," and it takes a greater momentum of "the Force" on the "light side" to conquer it. Jesus Christ is the go-to master with momentum on the light side. He has the office in spiritual hierarchy of "Lord and Savior" for a reason.

The apostle Paul speaks to this dichotomy of good and evil within us when he says, "For the good that I would I do not: but the evil which I would not, that I do" (Romans 7:19 KJV).

If you come from a background in Buddhism, you know that evil is the work of Mara, the temptress who comes in both male and female manifestations to seduce us away from the path. In Hinduism, there are many enemies of the soul mentioned in the Vedas, their Holy Scripture. The resisting or the succumbing to inner and outer habits of darkness has been our story on earth since the fall in the Garden of Eden. For me, the shark was a composite and symbol of this enemy, "the dweller."

A great deal of my work as a mystic and a minister has to do

---

[7] Dweller on the threshold is defined as, "A term sometimes used to designate the anti-self, the not-self, the synthetic self, the antithesis of the Real Self, the conglomerate of the self-created ego, ill conceived through the inordinate use of the gift of free will."

This definition was recorded in Mark L. Prophet and Elizabeth C. Prophet, *Saint Germain on Alchemy: Formulas for Self-Transformation* (Gardiner, Montana: SU Press, 1993), glossary.

with recognizing these patterns in myself and in the people I am trying to help.

MORE MYSTICAL EXPERIENCES

It was in Catholic elementary school that I fell in love with Jesus and Mother Mary and wanted to be close to them. I wanted to become a Catholic, but it was not possible for me. Back then, in this particular school, you had to have someone Catholic in your family to sponsor and support you. No one in my family was Catholic. I wanted to become a nun too and, for a time, was very serious about it.

When I told my father, he just looked at me and probably pondered, *How deep does this go?* This desire to be a nun was pointing to something deeper—an intuitive feeling of my soul's desire for greater dedication and maybe to the incarnations where I did lead a cloistered life as a nun.

As a young adult, I once again saw the surfacing of the mystical path in my study of Eastern religions and the practice of yoga. Once, when chanting and meditating, I briefly left my physical body, and as I looked down upon it from a distance, I knew for sure that I was not my body. I was in the observant mind, and I questioned again, "Who am I?"

My search came to the forefront of my life when who I AM in reality was revealed to me in the experience I had in 1978 at the Summit Lighthouse Conference in Pasadena that I've told you about. And then, when I heard about the path of the Bodhisattva[8] from the East, it resonated. It really resonated!

---

[8] "The Bodhisattva is one destined for Buddhahood and whose energy and power is directed toward enlightenment. Out of deep compassion for the plight of the world, the

CHART OF THE MIGHTY I AM PRESENCE

[1]The chart shows the relationship of the individual as a soul in a physical body to the divine self, providing a view of the nonphysical portion of our beings. It is a linear representation of what is actually a multidimensional manifestation of radiant, vibrating light energy.

The Chart of the Presence: In reality, the lower, middle, and upper figures in the chart are overlapping fields of energy vibrating at different frequencies, from denser physical energy to light energy vibrating at a higher rate.

The I AM Presence is represented by the top figure. It is

bodhisattva postpones nirvana until all beings have been liberated."

E. C. Prophet, *The Buddhic Essence: Ten Stages to Becoming a Buddha* (Montana: SU Press, 2009), 18.

the presence of God that is individualized in each of us. The multicolored body of light surrounding the presence is called the causal body, rotating spheres within spheres of radiant light energy.

The soul is represented by the lower figure in the chart. The light and energy of God descends to the soul through the I AM Presence over the crystal cord, the thin white line in the chart. Before it reaches the soul, it passes through "the Holy Christ self."

"The Holy Christ self", as mediator, steps down the tremendous energy of the I am Presence to a level where we can absorb it. The Christ self is our discriminating intelligence. It is the voice of conscience.

The flame in the center of your heart, in the lower figure, is called the threefold flame. It embodies the three aspects of the Trinity—power, wisdom, and love or Father, Son, and Holy Spirit. It is the part of our material existence that is pure spirit, and only that which is spirit can endure forever. Daily recognition of and devotion to the threefold flame leads to oneness with the Christ self. The soul must be fully bonded to the Christ before she can unite with the I AM Presence and make her ascension and become immortal.

GAIL HAWKINS

Gail Hawkins, who lived around the corner and up the street, was another of my very good friends. A fun thing we did was to spend all of Saturday at the local movie theater, "The Tower." We made sardine sandwiches, bought some greasy French fries from Ernie Copeland's store, got some popcorn later, and spent the entire day munching and watching what seemed like a zillion cartoons in color; reels of world and national news events in black and white; and two main features, either horror movies like *Dr. Frankenstein* or *The Thing* or Walt Disney movies like *Snow White and the Seven Dwarfs* or *Cinderella*. We had a ball! I guess we were about ten years old.

My parents and Gail's parents were friends, and we used to get together for New Years Eve. When we were about seven or eight, Gail and I would put on our mothers' makeup, fake fur coats, costume jewelry, and high heels and traipse around the house pretending to be movie stars. We also created a play we performed at midnight for the adults. They always looked forward to our little dramas. Our house would be filled with guests, her parents and mine. The pungent aroma of collard greens, black-eyed peas, and ham hocks was everywhere, while my grandma and father would be playing out their tunes on the baby grand piano in the family room. At midnight Gail and I would have all of their attention for our little skit. What a blast! That was our New Years tradition. In the words of William Shakespeare in *As You Like It*, "All the world's a stage, and men and women merely players. They have their exits and their entrances. And one man in his time plays many parts."

And so it was true of Gail and me in those performances. And so it is true for all of us in the great drama of life. This was another awakening to the idea of playing a role, putting it down, and then picking up another—another sign pointing the way.

Like you, I have come many times into the world to play different roles. I know I was in them to learn lessons, to overcome circumstances, and to win. Sometimes I did; sometimes I didn't. But for Gail and me, we always won because we created our own dramas with the outcomes we wanted. Life is not like that—a perfectly staged play with known outcomes. Some events might be preordained, but how we react to them is our choice. Fun was the aim of the games and little plays we created, and we always had lots of it.

Gail and Janet were the characters in my play as a child, and I was a character in theirs. As time went on, there were other scenes, grand and small, with different players, sets, and scenery. Who have been the performers in your life's drama? *Who have been the major and minor characters, the heroes, the villains, the stagehands? And who have been the directors?* The scenes are sometimes provided by karmic circumstance, and when we grow into our Christhood, we become "the director" for sure.

3

Growing Up

LATCHKEY KID

Between seven and nine years old, I was what you called a "latchkey kid." Both my parents worked, and so did my grandmother. No one got home until after five. I had the key and would come in each day after school to an empty house, turn on the TV, and do my homework. Sometimes I would dance to the Latin music of Celia Cruz and Tito Puente. When I did that, I pretended the house was full of people, and I was the hit of the party. One day, my father came home early and saw me dancing and talking to myself. I was *so* embarrassed. This *was my* private world, and he had seen a portion of it! It was like God himself had seen me. I wasn't doing anything wrong, but I felt exposed, found out.

Most weekday nights, I prepared the beginnings of a dinner meal. I broiled chicken or cooked hot dogs and sometimes fried cabbage. When my mother and grandmother got home, the main part of the dinner would be ready. My dad, a New York homicide detective, had to work all hours and often did not get home for dinner. They trusted I would be okay on my own. The neighborhood was relatively safe, and I had "eyes" on me, so they said. New Yorkers in general are independent go-getters. You had to be. Later, when I was a young adult, coming from the Bronx and working in Manhattan, I had to ride the El (elevated train) and then the subway. There were hundreds of us on those trains, swaying with their rhythm and holding on to brown, sweaty straps while at the same time managing to read the newspaper. The newspapers, except for *The Daily News,* were quite large in those days, and it became an art to know how to fold them and read them without poking someone in the face.

I was always on the lookout for pickpockets and perverts too. It was a real drag, but it kept me alert. It helped me to notice my surrounding, and I saw all kinds of people and noticed their moods and attitudes. I didn't dare stare at anyone though. It became an art to observe people without letting them see me do it. Later, these powers of observation assisted me in seeing the subtleties of my own motivations and behaviors.

Today I am a practical mystic and not always inwardly turned, as you would imagine a mystic to be—sitting in a lotus posture somewhere in the Himalayas meditating. I love people and very much care about them. I think that Harriet Tubman and Sojourner Truth were practical mystics too. I believe they had an intimate relationship with God to be able to lead slaves in their march to freedom through dangerous swamps at night. I try to lend a helping hand in the Buddhist tradition of the bodhisattva—one who hears the cries of the world and serves humanity. I got a good look at humanity riding the El and the buses and subways of the Bronx and Manhattan.

I got a good look at a lot of things walking to school every day as well. On one particular day, there was a crowd of people around the cellar area of an apartment building. I was curious and went over to see what was happening. An electrician had fallen from the wires and was lying dead on the concrete below. I was mesmerized by the vivid image of a man lying dead.

This picture of death became lodged in my subconscious and arose in me later when I was a young woman as a fear of dying young. I knew I had a mission, and this fear of an early death impelled me as a young person to find and fulfill it as quickly as possible.

Later in life, when working with a therapist, I found out that these kinds of incidents and even the death of a beloved pet can affect a child's feelings about death and carry over to adult life. It is an understanding about of which I think I am just beginning to scratch the surface. Imagine how one or two experiences of observing death can have such a profound effect. It begs the question, what other unrecalled intense experiences were impressed on my subconscious and unconscious that I don't remember but have had a profound effect on me as a young person and as an adult? Have you ever thought about this? Compelling, isn't it?

The ascended masters talk about the need for us to work on our psychology to understand why we do what we do, why we feel as we feel, and so on. It is integral to the work of rebuilding ourselves in the image of God and following the path of self-transformation, as taught by the ascended masters.[9]

As I grew older, Gail and Janet and I went our separate ways.

---

[9] Mark L. Prophet and Elizabeth C. Prophet, *The Path of Self-Transformation* (Gardiner, Montana: SU Press, 2000).

In the last few years, we've reconnected, along with other friends from our growing-up years. It feels good. Those childhood and young adult friendships are precious, and I am grateful for them. Janet has since passed on.

As a teen, I had not yet developed a strong identity. I was a little of my father and a little of my mother and probably a little of some other folks too. I very much wanted to please. Finding my uniqueness was my challenge as a child, adolescent, and young adult, and it was a trial and error process and quite painful. I was sorting out what characteristics I wanted to keep of my parents and which ones I wanted to discard without having fully established my own sense of self, my own person. The negative habit patterns I picked up from them and those I created myself were not my true self, my higher self, and I could in time let them go—things like criticism, lack of self worth, or fear of death.

I understand now that the negative behaviors I saw in them were not completely theirs either. They had internalized many of them from their parents unwittingly. We all appropriate the good, bad, and ugly from those close to us. The good, as virtues, ascends to our causal body and is stored there as our "treasure in heaven."[10] (The causal body of colored spheres depicted in the Chart of the Mighty I AM Presence.) This is the masters' teaching. The ugly, as I explained, goes to the unconscious and subconscious, forming the components of the dweller on the threshold or the "not self."

---

[10] "Lay up not for yourselves treasures upon earth where moth and rust doth corrupt, and thieves break through and steal t lay up for yourselves treasures in heaven where nether moth nor rust doth corrupt, and where thieves do not break through nor steal: For where your treasure is there will be our heart also" (Matthew 6:19–21 KJV).

It's like the Dr. Jekyll and Mr. Hyde syndrome[11], though, for most of us, it's not carried out to that extreme.

There were very good characteristics I inherited from my parents as well—among them directness, a good work ethic, and caring about and serving people.

The soul picks up both the positive and the negative traits of those close to her and has the opportunity to shed the negative ones as she evolves. She, the soul, is the wisest part of our evolving being. Your Christ self, and mine, *is* the evolved being.

ENERGY MUST HAVE SOMEWHERE TO GO

Another condition that affected my inner world and personality was the fact that I had no siblings. This made me unfamiliar with sibling banter and rivalry, and I remained very sensitive and slow to develop the ability to give and take teasing without being offended. At this age, I did not know that only the human ego could be offended and not the real self. I did not have a rough exterior or the skill for stinging comebacks when "being poked fun at" or criticized. Nor could I completely reject what my friends and classmates teased me about. I couldn't tell if my they really meant what they were saying or were just being kids. I would withdraw emotionally.

Again, I learned that energy must have somewhere to go. And since I did not defend myself from what was hurled at me, it

---

[11] Dr. Jekyll was a physician who turned into Mr. Hyde, a murderer at night. Jekyll and Hyde people can love and be gentle sometimes and then turn angry, harsh, and sometimes violent at other times.

Robert Louis Stevenson, *The Strange Case of Dr. Jekyll land Mr. Hyde* (England: Longmans Green and Co., 1886).

landed on me. You see, either I had to hurl it back or consciously reject it, or it would and did stick on me like globs of mud on a wall that, by their very weight, sank deeper and deeper into the well of my unconscious, lurking there for a time to jump out without my conscious permission. I was often too shocked or hurt to directly reject them so I retained these energies and they began to form a pattern that colored my thoughts and feelings. That fact affected my relationships.

Looking back to the rearing of my own children I see how some of those patterns may have influenced my parenting. I'm certain that I said things and made choices on their behalf that I wouldn't have made except for these hidden influences.

I remember an example of this pattern. It was an occasion when I came into a classroom as a substitute for a sixth grade teacher and the kids laughed and declared, "Ha, ha, we got a substitute. You won't control us!"

I respond, "I have been a teacher for many years. And, yes, I will."

And then the war began. The students wouldn't sit down when asked; they talked back, socialized, and threw insults, not just at me but also at each other. I threatened them and called security, huffed and puffed—their dwellers battling with my dweller and vice versa.

This tug-of-war between dwellers was evidence of the subconscious pattern I'm talking about. I feared I would lose control, and I did—because I was moved from the center of my being and reacted out a need to control. I set up an argument right from the beginning that we did not have to have, and I was not conscious of it until later. My prideful reaction was the sprouting of a seed of an unconscious pattern and a component of my "dweller on the threshold."

By the way, as soon as I became fully aware of how I'd set up the situation, I didn't repeat it again. I did not want to awaken anyone's dweller, especially those of thirty-five preteens.

REALIZATIONS

We all have this stuff of the unreal self in layers. One layer gets peeled off and then another and then another. It is the work of the mystic in tandem with a master. When I see a layer as it peels off, it is often a surprise. *My God, I didn't see that! Wow! What a revelation!*

I had a confrontation with a colleague some years back, in which I was quite direct and unkind. Yet self-righteously, I felt I was being truthful. I used to run into this individual, and I was always friendly, as I really held nothing against her. Some years later, I realized how unkind I had been, although I had felt justified. I sensed she had been hurt by my words, and it presents me now with some unfinished business to take care of. Sometimes you do not realize until months or years later the affects of your words on another person.

After the encounter with these sixth graders, I felt like I had just gone through a terrible and unnecessary battle, and no one had won but the "dark force" and our "dwellers."

What I know now is that the unwinding and unraveling of these deep-seated negative patterns of thinking and behavior require the help of a master who, in most cases, has "been there, done that" in one of their many lifetimes. Whether the help comes

from the master Jesus, Krishna, Buddha, or your inner Holy
Christ self or Mighty I AM presence, it is a work to be done in
partnership with God.

Our human predicament in our march toward wholeness goes
all the way back to the Garden of Eden. The ascended masters
teach that the Garden of Eden was a mystery school of the Great
White Brotherhood.[12] "White" doesn't refer to race, but to the
white light surrounding the saints—the halo often depicted in
classical paintings. Eden was a school where we were taught the
mysteries of God and initiated into the higher truths. Because
we failed our test of obedience by eating the apple and partaking
of the Tree of Good and Evil (relativity), we are where we are
today, in a world of relativity grappling with our karma. Life ain't
always easy.

Let us understand, God has a right to test us!

The mystery school of Eden is open again by the grace of Lord
Maitreya. It is available to enter by his grace and our striving.[13]

More and more, I feel myself transcending former aspects
of my self—ideas, attitudes, and ways of behaving—as layers of
unreality drop from me. Yesterday I understood something, and
today I am applying it everywhere. The tomorrows will uncover

[12] "The Great White Brotherhood is a spiritual order of Western saints and Eastern adepts
who have reunited with the living spirit of God and who comprise the heavenly hosts."

Elizabeth Clare Prophet, *The Great White Brotherhood in the Culture, History and Religion
of America* (Gardiner, Montana: SU Press, 1984), Introduction.
[13] On May 31,1984, Jesus Christ announced in a dictation through the messenger Elizabeth
Clare Prophet that Lord Maitreya was dedicating the Royal Teton Ranch as the place
prepared for the reestablishment of his mystery school in this age.

Elizabeth C. Prophet, "Maitreya: A Study in Christhood by the Great Initiator" in
Pearls of Wisdom, Book I, bound volume (Gardiner, Montana: SU Press, May 1984), "Pearl
31, Beloved Jesus the Christ."

more to shed and more golden nuggets of truth to digest and apply until I AM Awake, like the Buddha.[14]

Some things I am not ready to let go of yet, like my caffeine-filled matcha green tea. But for right now, I am waking up. And as I wake up, I know with all of my heart that you and I are truly made in His image. Jesus knew this about us. He said that what he did we can do likewise.[15] God was in Jesus, and God is in me and in you. If I can do likewise, with Jesus's help, so can you. This is his true teaching: that we can be like him. The apostle Paul said, "Christ in you the hope of glory." In Colossians 27:1, we read, "To whom God would make known what is the riches of glory of this mystery among the Gentiles; which is Christ in you, the hope of glory" (KJV).

The idea of a perfect man or woman having been born only once and not having gone through the fires of trial and error over many incarnations, making mistakes, and then correcting them, with deep soul searching is erroneous and idolatrous. Jesus was the example of a God man, an overcomer. Yet even he with all of his spiritual attainment had to learn lessons growing up. The Bible says that he learned obedience by the errors he made. "Though he were a Son, yet learned he obedience by the things which he suffered" (Hebrews 5:8 KJV).

---

[14] "I AM Awake!" said the Buddha when asked by a disciple, "How are you?"

[15] "Verily, verily I say unto you, He that believeth on me, the works that I do shall he do also; and grater works than these shall he do; because I go unto my Father" (The Gospel of John 14:12 KJV).

27

FIRST GRADE

An indelible experience I had in first grade was to stick with me into my adult years. I was six years old. It was 1948, and it was my first day of school and I would be attending the Catholic school about seven blocks from my house. I was wearing a navy blue uniform, a white blouse, and brown and white Buster Brown shoes. My hair was plaited in three braids. I was very excited and a little fearful too, anxious to see whom some of my new friends would be and what my teacher would be like.

We were lined up in the hallway, boys and girls together. Sister, wearing a long black habit, was inspecting the line when a white hanky fell from her sleeve. I stepped out of line, picked it up, and handed it to her, happy I was being of some help. The response I got was so unexpected. She lit into me as if I had done the unimaginable and severely scolded me in front of my classmates. I felt shattered, but I did not show it. This was in the morning, my first day of school, before class even started. I never told my parents.

As I thought about it in later years, I guessed Sister would probably justify her behavior as having something to do with keeping order and showing that she was boss that first day. We were fifty kids after all. She no doubt wanted to exercise her authority. But as a child, I did not understand. I was not used to being criticized for a kind act. So powerful was the put-down, so sensitive was I that, as a young adult, it was hard for me to "step out of line" even to defend my principles. I often kept my feelings to myself. It was the wrong thing for her to do. To me, in my child's mind, she represented the authority figure, maybe even

God and was at least a person of trust. It was a huge negative. She had just wasted me.

I was put out of Catholic school after fifth grade because the school was overcrowded, and I was not a Catholic. I didn't go to church at all from then on and didn't show any interest in religion until I took up Eastern religions in my twenties.

I wonder today if that experience in Catholic school had something to do with my rejection of religion for all those years. I sense that I didn't reject God, but God did get a back seat for a while.

My Feelings Begin To Flow

It was an ascended master who came to my assistance many years later after I'd had that childhood trauma in Catholic school. This was the same ascended master whose book I had read and who, I think, during a dictation given by the messenger, provided the spiritual sponsorship for me to experience my indwelling Christ. That master was Kuthumi Lal Singh.[16] You might ask me how do I know this. I simply know it.

In a previous lifetime, he was Saint Francis of Assisi, who Jesus instructed to rebuild his church. The churches at that time were corrupt. Francis took him literally and started to rebuild churches. He took the vow of poverty and founded the Order of

---

[16] Kuthumi is the ascended master who serves with Jesus in the Office of World Teacher. Some of his earthly lifetimes include architect of the Egyptian empire; Pythagoras, 582-c, 507 BC; Balthazar, one of the three wise men (the three Magi); Saint Francis of Assisi; and Shah Jahan, who built the Taj Mahal.

E. C. Prophet, compiled by Annice Booth, *The Masters and Their Retreats* (Gardiner, Montana: SU Press), 169–73.

Franciscan Friars. He was canonized as a saint two years after his death at the age of forty-four. Saint Francis is known for his love of Jesus and his gentleness and ability to communicate with animals.

One day, about forty-nine years after having that childhood experience with the nun, I was sitting in the Court of King Arthur, the chapel at the Royal Teton Ranch headquarters of the Summit Lighthouse. Right at that time, an opportunity for kindness was presented to me. Reverend Marilyn Barrick was delivering a lecture on psychology at the podium. She started to cough and was having a time of it. I was sitting in the back of the chapel concerned that no one was getting her water. So I went to get her some water and walked from the back of the chapel up to the podium and handed it to her.

Unlike the nun who scolded me for picking up her hanky, the reverend accepted my kindness and was grateful.

When I returned to my seat, I began to cry. I could not stop the tears from flowing down my cheeks and felt I might be making quite a scene, so I left the chapel and walked out to the tree farm where I "let it rip."

The tears flowed; the dam of many years had broken, releasing the waters of a childhood trauma. Dr. Barrick's acceptance of my kind act was transmuting the nun's rejection and unkindness, and its imprint on my soul from years ago. I did not know why I was crying. In other words, at the time, I could not pinpoint any particular experience. But I could feel, and that was the point. I could feel! And I believe that that particular record of pain had been cleared and, with it, other similar records.

We all have many records of betrayal from childhood. I had my share, and after the experience with the nun, there were others on into adulthood where I kept my feelings to myself. It made me unhealthy and emotionally crippled at the time. But now, with this release, I was freer, and I gave great glory to God!

I knew this release was a blessing from the master Kuthumi. He is the one who drew me to the summit in the first place. It was his book I picked up off the shelf that day in a New Age bookstore in Richmond and it was the first book I read published by the Summit Lighthouse. The name of the book is *Studies of the Human Aura*. The first time I heard a live dictation by Mrs. Prophet, it was from the same master, Kuthumi. Rev. Marilyn Barrick was also a student of Kuthumi's, and it was he, I am sure, who was inspiring her lecture that day.

As I have said before, energy has to have somewhere to go. It doesn't evaporate. If it is not released, it is stored as a record in my subconscious. Learning how to release it appropriately takes mastery—mastery over my emotions, thoughts, and actions. We see evidence everyday of people who exhibit the Dr. Jekyll and Mr. Hyde syndrome that I mentioned and who release it inappropriately—the quiet man who screams at his boss, the unassuming person who kills his girlfriend, and the teacher who blows up at her students. This is stored energy building to disastrous consequences. These feelings can be lodged in the body and can count for so many of the illnesses we have as well. There are many articles and books that speak of the connection between the mind, the emotions, and the body.

Surely I have had other similar experiences that I don't remember or have repressed. Any cover up of my true feelings gives me over time a karmic pattern to overcome. It takes time and space to unravel this. It's like peeling an onion. One layer

31

comes off and then another and another. Layer by layer, they come off. It's a process of divesting oneself of what is negative and harmful.

I needed help in healing myself. I could never have made such a contact as I had made with my Holy Christ self in Pasadena in 1978 if it had not been for the messenger Elizabeth Clare Prophet and the ascended masters. It was a gift to me. You can struggle for years on your own or with a teacher who is not a true master. I accepted my path then and there with the ascended masters who are a part of God's hierarchy in this Age of Aquarius.

In this age, God, when times are dark, always sends His messengers to remind us of who we are and to provide us with the opportunity for reconnecting to Him personally. Jesus, Moses, Lao Tzu, Buddha, founders of the major religions of the world, and others were the messengers sent in their times. Mark and Elizabeth Prophet were modern-day messengers who came to initiate a revolution in higher consciousness. As a caveat I will add that there are very high souls who are at the point of their ascension who may not have heard of the ascended masters or the messengers. Often these souls have come to know them in the spiritual retreats where they have had instruction and learned to make invocation to the flames of God—the violet flame of freedom, for example, given to us by the master Saint Germain,[17]

---

[17] The violet flame, brought to our awareness by Saint Germain as a gift from God, is the seventh ray aspect of the Holy Spirit, the scared fire that transmutes the cause, effect, record, and memory of sin or negative karma.

Mark L. Prophet and Elizabeth C. Prophet, *Saint Germain on Alchemy: Formulas for Self-Transformation* (Gardiner, Montana: Summit University Press), 1993, glossary.

For more information on Saint Germain: Mark L. Prophet Mark and Elizabeth C. Prophet, *The Masters and Their Retreats,* compiled and edited by Annice Booth (Gardiner, Montana: SU Press, 2003), 312–22.

the yellow flame of illumination, the pink flame of love, and so forth. When you look at a colored version of the chart of the Presence you will see in the upper part of the chart seven concentric rings of color. Each ring represents a sphere that expresses attributes of God that we can invoke. When we make the invocation the light descends as rays. Some people have a great deal of mastery on one or several of these rays and there you see genius. Paul the apostle, for instance, had great mastery on the green ray of preaching the truth and of healing. People in positions of leadership generally have mastery of the attributes of the blue ray. As I have said, these advanced souls who may not be aware of the messengers or the ascended masters are nearing their ascension and only require the knowledge and application of one of the rays. It is usually the violet ray of transmutation to get rid of their remaining karma. This work happens in the retreats where they travel at night in their etheric bodies. When they awaken they may or may not remember the experience. Please see the glossary in *Saint Germain on Alchemy* already cited in previous footnotes on the etheric body and etheric retreats and other books of the Prophets for the colored chart of the Presence.)

I was healed of that childhood record that day in the Court of King Arthur. It was a beginning. I have continued to use the mantra, "I AM (God in me) is a being of violet fire, I AM (God in me) is the purity God desires." It is the antidote to many of my repressed emotional experiences, When I use this mantra and others, the violet energy of the Holy Spirit descends and erases the cause, effect, record and memory in my unconscious and subconscious of painful karmic circumstances one by one, over time, but not all. The masters tell us some traumas in life require facing and must be understood. Once that happens, we can let them go. Into the flame they go! Into the violet transmuting flame! What a blessing! You can do this too! (See Mark and Elizabeth Clare Prophet, The Science of the Spoken Word: (Gardiner, Montana, SU)Press, 2004)

As my divine personality began to envelope me more and more, I gained the esteem and self-worth to be outspoken without requiring agreement. I could express how I really felt about something and respond appropriately to someone's hurtful behavior. I learned how not to withdraw when someone said or acted in a way I did not like. I became outspoken in fact. Being offended about anything started to fade, and with Jesus I would affirm inwardly, *what is that to thee, follow thou me.*[18] In other words, if you have a goal, keep your eyes on it and follow the teacher who will lead you to it. And, don't pay attention to what is not essential to it.

I have been using the violet flame for over forty years, and it has helped me and is helping me heal many of my relationships, past and present. It is truly an elixir from the heart of the beloved master Saint Germain.

---

[18] **"What is that to thee? Follow thou Me. For what is it to thee whether a man be this or that, or say or do thus or thus? Thou hast no need to answer for others, but thou must give an answer for thyself"** (Gospel of John 21:22 KJV).

4

Karma and Reincarnation[19]

"Karma is energy/consciousness in action. It is the law of cause and effect and retribution. Also called the Law of the Circle that decrees that whatever we do comes full circle to our doorstep for resolution. This law necessitates the soul's reincarnation until all karmic cycles are balanced. Thus from lifetime to lifetime man determines his fate by his actions, including his thoughts, feelings, words and deeds."[20]

You have heard the adage, "What goes around, comes around," or, "Cast your bread on waters for you shall find it after many days" (Ecclesiastes 11:1 KJV). Every erg of energy misused in fear, doubt, anger, hatred, and all the negatives, as well as positive emotions, actions, and thoughts return to our doorstep. What, pray tell, do we think when the energy returns? The enlightened thought is, *Aha! I am responsible for this and I must balance it!* The

---

[19] Saint Germain teaches the accelerated path of transmutation of the karma by the *violet flame of the Holy Spirit* and transcending of the rounds of rebirth through the path of individual Christhood leading to the ascension demonstrated by Jesus.

[20] Reincarnation and karma: Mark L. Prophet and Elizabeth Prophet, *Saint Germain on Alchemy: Formulas for Self-Transformation* (Gardiner, Montana: SU Press, 1993), glossary.

G. De Purucker, *The Esoteric Tradition* volume 2 (California: Theosophical University Press, 1973).

irresponsible response is to blame. When the good karma returns as opportunities, rewarding relationships, and other blessings, I give glory to God. Actually, all karma is good because it's a teacher designed to help us grow and increase in our mastery and spirituality. The law of reincarnation, on the other hand, is the law of cosmos that mercifully gives us the time, space, and opportunity to balance this energy called "negative" karma.

Have you ever wondered why you have the family you have? Or what is the difference between a Mother Theresa, who some regard as a saint, and a person who aspires for worldly success through fame and fortune?

Desire leads us to fulfill much of what we fulfill in life. There are no accidents or coincidences, and we are born into our families and situations, races, and cultures out of our desire to learn specific lessons and master specific circumstances. Some are born to be saintly because they desire to give their all to God and His children. Others want to complete projects left undone; some have to experience difficult economic karma. And some come into the world with a mental or physical disability that is designed to expand their family and community's capacity to love them. Some come accumulating great wealth because perhaps in a previous incarnation they suffered great lack of material wealth.

I cannot judge anyone's circumstance because I am only seeing a few frames of a life when there may be millions. Every person has a story and that story goes way back in time and stretches way forward into the future. There is a story about a man that illustrates this. I don't remember where I heard it or perhaps I read it somewhere. Perhaps it's familiar to you. This middle-aged man was on a subway with his three children. His appearance was disheveled, his clothes wrinkled, his hair uncombed. His children were running around making a racket and disturbing people. A lady came up to him and scolded him for not attending to them properly. Other passengers rolled their eyes because they too were disturbed. The man slowly looked up at the lady and said: "I'm sorry, I've been at the hospital all night. My wife just died. I'm heart broken t and not quite handling this situation very well." Immediately upon hearing the full story, all perceptions of the man and of what was happening changed. At the beginning we only see one frame or snap shot of the situation. Now, with the understanding of the previous one (his wife had just died) we gain a clearer view. We feel sorry for the man. We understand his inattention to his children. We have compassion. And, we come to understand that in judging a person or incident we often don't see the whole picture.

So the great master says, "Don't Judge".

> If we do not like our circumstances in life, we can change them in time. All of us, by our vision and drive, can overcome challenges; earn virtues; and become successful, spiritually, materially, and emotionally. Success is not exclusive to a few. After all, *Jesus came that we might have life and have it more abundantly,* John 10:10 KJV. It requires persistent application of heart, mind, and soul to God's laws and an attitude of responsibility and victory. If I can face my experiences with the love and wisdom that life is intended to teach me, I move a notch closer to becoming my real self, my Christ self.

WE CHOOSE OUR FAMILIES

We choose our families in consultation with a board of ascended masters called the Karmic Board.[21] The experiences I had with my chosen family growing up gave me a sense of the unity of my own soul with the souls of all others. I could not articulate, nor was I aware of, the concepts of the path of mysticism or "personal Christhood" or even "soul." But I felt a deep connection to the people I met through my parents and their friends, the black community, the Jews I went to school with and the Puerto Ricans in my neighborhood and others from Central and South America. It made it easy for me to be comfortable with people from all over the world. I sensed there was something that bound us together, strong and more important than our races, our environments, and our languages. It was our common human predicament and our origin in God and destiny to return. And this is what I felt. It came from a deep place in me, and it flowed from the experiences my parents afforded me; from their friends and acquaintances; and, no doubt, from my own varied past incarnations.

I had an experience once at the airport in Minneapolis. I was coming from Montana on my way home to Maryland. There was a woman from somewhere in the Middle East sitting near me. She was by herself and so was I. I was curious about her. She had a regal bearing and was lost in her thoughts as if something was

---

[21] "The Lords of Karma: ... Every soul must pass before the Lords of Karma who sit on a Karmic Board before and after each incarnation on earth, receiving their assignments and karmic allotment for each lifetime beforehand and the review of their performance at each conclusion."

Mark L. Prophet and Elizabeth Prophet, *Saint Germain on Alchemy* (Gardiner, Montana: SU Press, 1985), glossary.

disturbing her. I felt comfortable in her presence and we started up a conversation. It turned out she was from Egypt going to visit her estranged son and she didn't know how he would react to her visit. She was nervous about it and so we talked. She said her husband would not have let her go on this trip if it wasn't for the fact that she had her own money and wasn't dependent on him. I could tell by her jewelry and the beautiful clothing she wore that she had money. She appeared to be in her late fifties. She asked me if I would get her some coffee and I went off to get it. I don't remember her name. It was simply a contact of the moment yet, she felt like a sister. All the differences in culture and language were unimportant. We were just two women, one sharing her heart and the other listening. We were comfortable with one another. The concern she had for her son and their relationship was a universal concern most mothers have. I took her son's name and prayed with her for him to receive her graciously. We finally said goodbye and went to our respective flights. I never saw her again nor did I expect to ever see her again. Has something like this ever happened to you? You make a one-time connection with a stranger that is not superficial. Maybe for me, this short reunion was with someone I'd known before in a past life. I felt I had known her.

I was born into my family because I needed them, and they needed me. No situation is perfect on the surface. But this one was definitely the right one for me. Karma and reincarnation are precise calculations. The exact configurations have to be there with the people we need to meet—the associations, friends, and (so-called) enemies. The people I found in my orbit were not accidentally there. My family and their friends, whose friendships

I enjoyed, were assets in my quest for a deeper understanding of life. They were examples I could imitate, as they unearthed memories of other times and excellence in their present professions. They gave context to my spiritual trek. This time around, in this incarnation, I was born into the Jones family.

MY MOTHER

My mother, Edith Jones, was a tall olive brown woman, a social worker and also an accomplished artist. Under her sometimes-gruff nature she had a heart of gold and would do anything for you. Her influence brought me back to the love of art, painting and drawing, something that was a central part of my experience in past lives. I paint some today. When I don't or cannot because of other projects, I find myself at various art museums to just keep a toe in. I cannot name these past lives specifically, but I have the sense of having been a painter and writer of the Spanish language in past centuries. The Spanish language has a dear memory for me. It has been the gateway to my balancing karma with others.

My mother had a wonderful vocation—helping folks to adopt babies. Her work took her to many projects all over New York City and up and down many staircases visiting prospective couples. She was a hard worker and a good mother in the traditional sense. She did all of the right things—kept me clean and well fed, helped keep a roof over my head, and took me shopping at Bloomingdales. I know she loved me very much. I was strong-willed, and she had a hard time disciplining me when I was little.

I did not like her very much either when I was little; after all, she was the main competition for my father's love. It wasn't until I was an adult that I really began to appreciate my mother. It wasn't that she was so much a different person then but because she was female, human, and imperfect and made the best of her life circumstances. And as much as I loved my father, I began to see some of her challenges being married to him. I started to observe her from a woman's point of view, rather than a child's. Nonetheless, she was his childhood sweetheart and first love, and he was hers. And that kept them glued together and me secure in their love.

My mother appreciated the outer things—how you looked, what you wore, how much money you made. A lot of this had to do with the economic times and the social class she grew up in. She and her sisters Ruth and Lillian grew up in the Cranford Casino, where her father and mother were the caretakers. She was exposed to rich white people as a child and learned to appreciate how they lived. When I was sixteen, my mother asked me if I wanted a cotillion (a coming-out party for young women to introduce them to society). Or, would I rather go to Mexico on the Experiment in International Living (- a global language imersion program.)

I chose to go to Mexico instead of participating in the cotillion., My mother cheered. She looked down on middle-class blacks trying to imitate whites—and poorly at that, she thought. Her soul needed security, and she sought it materially.

This emphasis on outer things became a real friction between us. She always wanted me to look pretty. I guess it's understandable for a mother to feel like that about her only daughter. But it was more than that. She wanted me to be the center of attention, and it made me feel uncomfortable.

I knew even then that, contrary to societal beliefs, physical appearances were important but not all that important. Yet I had to acknowledge that it's often the most important thing for a lot of people and a ticket of acceptance in many circles.

I don't want to be smug about it. I had that asset of physical attractiveness, so it was not something that was a goal for me. Like most things in life, it came with its ups and downs. The downside was people often did not really see me as a person. Some women were jealous, and I attracted unwanted sexual interest from some men. I did fit into many circles, so overall, in retrospect, I am very grateful for that asset.

You could say that my mother reaffirmed what most of the world admired. I admired good looks too. That's the truth. I was not immune. I do not judge my mother. By contrast, she actually reinforced my desire to look beyond the apparent.

Many years later, my parents had an apartment in the same complex my present husband and I lived in with our son Michael. One afternoon, my father called and told us to come over immediately. When we got there, my mom was on the floor, and the medics were attending her. My husband was asked to give her mouth-to-mouth resuscitation.

I asked my dad what had happened. He said she'd come out of the bedroom and had told him she was very tired and asked if she could just lie on the couch for a while.

She passed away right then and there. After Mom died, my dad moved in with us. I remember going to clean up their vacated apartment. As I cleared the books from some shelves in the kitchen, I saw an old cookbook written by some friends of hers from New Jersey.

Just as I took it off the shelf, my mom, in the body of a vibrant, happy young woman, appeared next to me in a flash. The experience was brief and magnificent. I believe she was letting me know she was okay and really happy. She passed from this life when she was eighty-six and my father at ninety-four.

After he passed, I had a dream that I was helping both of them get on a plane to go somewhere they were trying to get to. This was another reinforcement for me that life is on a continuum and that the stage called death is just a pause before a cycle of new beginnings. The plane they were catching was taking them somewhere higher on their path, to one of the many mansions prepared by the Father. There are etheric retreats of the brotherhood where souls go for learning.[22] The point here is that dreams are often real experiences in other dimensions and not just dreams. My parents were moving up in their journey homeward, and I was helping them.

My mother revived the love for art and service that's part of my spiritual path today. But it was my grandmother in particular who provided me with a powerful example of motherhood. Her strength, discipline, love, and especially her calm evenhandedness nurtured my soul. She was the rock in my world.

MY GRANDMOTHER AND HER HUSBAND CHARLIE

---

[22] The etheric plane is the highest plane in the dimension of matter, a plane that is as concrete and real (even more so) than the physical plane in a dimension and consciousness above physical awareness. The ascended masters have their retreats on this plane.

   Mark L Prophet and Elizabeth C. Prophet, *Saint Germain on Alchemy* (Gardiner, Montana: SU Press, 1993), glossary, "etheric plane."

Most of us have that special person we look up to, one who understands us best and is patient with us and who we trust completely. If it's not a family member, it could be the school bus driver or security person or the mailman or teacher. For me, it was my grandmother—Augusta Patterson, better known by all as "Ma Pat." She was an example to me of patience and love. But most of all, she provided an archetype of God's love as Mother that I needed in order to be able to recognize and love my teacher when I met her.

My teacher is Elizabeth Clare Prophet. We call her Ma or Mother because of her devotion to God as mother. Even though I had a great relationship with my dad and later with my mom, I could not trust that he would always be there. His job took him away from home a lot, and sometimes when I needed him to intercede between my mother, and me he was not there. For me, the person I could trust to be there was Ma Pat, my father's mother and a mother to many who loved her.

My dear grandmother left her home in Omaha, Nebraska, in the late 1800s when she was fourteen years old to attend a boarding school. She said her mother told her she sent her away to protect her from a rumored Indian raid. It sounded a little strange to me, and I wish I had asked her more about it before she passed.

Ma Pat was my rock. Every weekend, we would sit together and watch the Perry Como Show. She loved Perry Como. She also loved watching the Dinah Shore and Nat King Cole shows. These were popular entertainers of the '50s.

When my parents vacationed, Ma Pat would be the one to take care of me. I remember once, we were at our summer home in Sag Harbor, and I tripped over a rock and hurt my leg. I was about eleven or twelve. Ma Pat was a big woman with big arms, and she had to half carry and half drag me to the closest house, the Hawkins house—parents of my childhood friend Gail. I was crying, and we were struggling. She was her calm self in contrast to me. And that was they way she was. We finally got there, and I got bandaged. I still have the scar.

Ma Pat was a Capricorn, and all of her life she had challenges. She had married my grandfather, a half black, half Potawatomie Indian, who died just after my father was born. She then married a Patterson. But the marriage didn't last. Her birthday was Christmas. There were great celebrations and joyous fun in our home at that time of year. Ma Pat and my father would play the baby grand in the family room, and there would be lots of food and guests coming and going all day till late in the night.

When my grandma died, the light and joy of Christmas went out in our home. After her death, there were no more live Christmas trees with red, gold, and green bulbs; silver tinsel; fake snow; and the smell of pine needles. No longer were "Jingle Bells," "Rudolph the Red Nose Reindeer," and others festive melodies sung or played on the big baby grand. And there were no more parties or New Years plays with my friend Gail to entertain guests. There were no more guests! It was as if she'd carried all of that joy and festivity inside of her, and when she left, she had taken it all with her.

It must have devastated me. I think I was in shock for many years. I did not mourn then. I was twelve years old.

The last time I saw my grandma was in her bed at home; her

big body frame had shrunk almost to a skeleton. I could clearly see her bones. Cancer had eaten her up. I shed no tear.

It wasn't until I started to write these memoirs that I began to deeply reconnect with her. I re-experienced my feelings around the event of her illness and the love and joy and reassurance my grandma had always given me, and then I began to mourn. Recently, I had a dream in which I was able to tell her how much I loved her and thank her for her loving, tender care of me. It was a profoundly precious moment of spiritual connection between her soul and mine. God always provides an experience or message of affirmation of truth and resolution to the soul. He had provided that for my soul.

MY FATHER AND HIS BUDDIES

My father gave the spiritual and emotional support required for me to feel free to follow my path. He was not aware of my spiritual yearnings until later in life, and even then, he never let on that he really understood them. More than anything, my dad loved me unconditionally. When I was out of college and back from Europe, wondering what I was going to do now, he suggested I pursue a career in teaching Spanish. Spanish was my language from another incarnation, and as I told you, studying and teaching it helped me to fulfill a certain mission and balance a lot of karma.

My dad and I had very deep ties. We could sit and talk about anything. He loved the intellectual world of ideas, languages, philosophy, and sports. I was a good swimmer, and we used to swim together a lot. Both of us were good swimmers.

My father grew up in Omaha, Nebraska. His father, Charlie died soon after he was born and left a widow and young boy to do the best they could in hard times. When my dad was eight years old, he had a paper route and a dog that pulled his sled on the route. The dog he got from an old Native American man. He persuaded him to give it to him in exchange for doing small jobs. The dog was past his prime and no longer useful to this man. He wasn't very healthy either, but my father took care of it and nursed it back to health.

This man told my father, "You are not worth anything much, being neither black nor white nor fully Indian. You will have to make a name for yourself and prove your worth." Quite a remark to make to a young boy, is it not?

What that man said made a deep impression on my father. He told me so. One could look at the comment as cruel, or one could see it as the impetus for my father's striving for excellence. He chose to strive for excellence. In 1936, he was in the tryouts for shot put for the Olympic games. He attended Lincoln University in Pennsylvania, an all-black men's college at the time, where he also coached football. He later attended New York University, where he earned a bachelor's of science in physical education. Physical Education.

His mother said that, when he left Minnesota for NY University, the only things he took with him were his fishing pole, camping gear, and flint knife. He was definitely a country boy and carried that spirit everywhere throughout his life. He played tennis for the Negro Tennis League, traveling the United States in competitive games and winning hundreds of trophies.

He pursued a career in the New York Police Department, where he climbed the ladder to become a lieutenant, one of the first black lieutenants. He was recognized as an outstanding and honest cop and got his picture on the cover of the New York *Daily News* for apprehending a dishonest one.

When he retired from the police department, he became a special agent for the National Board of Fire Underwriters in New York. Still later, he served as deputy coordinator in the Police Community Relations Unit in the State Division of Human Rights in New York.

When he finally fully retired, he purchased a boat and called it the *Soledad* (the Solitary One). He studied with the Power Squadron IV, New York City, and earned the ranks of navigator and captain. He and my mother traveled all of the inner waterways between Florida and Canada and eventually navigated the 313 miles or so to the Bahamas, where they lived on the boat for several months.

He was an avid chess player and studied chess and Spanish up to his death at age ninety-four. He was a member of many associations—Alpha Phi Alpha fraternity, the Guardians, a black police fraternity, the National Association for the Advancement of Colored People (NAACP), International Association of Chiefs of Police, and the Honor Legion of the New York City Police Department, International Association of Arson Investigators, and others.

My father was an example of a person who was always studying to improve his knowledge. He charted his own course, and that course was set by what he brought with him from other incarnations and reinforced by the Native American in Omaha many years ago. For sure, that Indian struck a profound nerve when he told him he was neither black nor white nor Indian and would have to prove himself. And such is often true—a person who appears to be an enemy or cruel turns out to be a teacher who spurs us on. These people provide our turning points and are catalysts. God bless them!

I learned the most about teaching from a senior teacher who was responsible for my evaluation. She was quite unfair to me in some ways and always on my case. I had to perform. She was dishonest about an evaluation she gave me and the following year, with persuasion, she had decided to teach at a different school. I will always be grateful to her in any case because she helped me to improve my skill in teaching.

A story my dad told me that stands out and I want to share is so indicative of his character. It was early in his police career, and he was a rookie in Harlem. One day, he was on his beat in uniform, and some pranksters threw water out of a third-story window on his head.

His response was, "Hey guys, give me a break. I'm just a

rookie, new on the job. You shouldn't treat me like this." And he laughed.

From that day on, because of his humility and good nature, he made some friends who watched out for him and gave him tips about the "bad" guys.

I soaked up that good-natured spirit. I have it! And I can relate to just about anybody. My father taught me to always say hello to people who addressed me and not to be stuck up. Unbeknown to me, when I was little, he had the winos and the number runners who hung out on the corner of our block watching out for me while I walked to school each day.

Although fair-skinned, he always identified as black, even when they called him Indian Jones during his college football days. He was very much a part of the black community and his congenial spirit brought him many friends from many races and all walks of life. He played chess with Mr. Turner, a white neighbor who lived in Bridge Hampton in a cabin without electricity and running water. He ate roasted pig each year with another Mr. Turner, a black farmer who also lived in Bridge Hampton. While playing chess, he checkmated many a judge, lawyer, and doctor in the black middle-class enclave of Sag Harbor Hills where we had a summer home.

He tutored his good friend Boney on the GED. Boney lived up the street from our house in the Bronx. He was a short burly man who worked as a train engineer (conductor) for the New York Subway system. He had a great talent and strong hands and used to give my dad massages. My dad later introduced him to some of his judge, lawyer, and doctor friends in Sag Harbor. He then gained a clientele he never dreamed of.

Some years later, when Boney was home in bed dying, family all gathered around, my dad just happened to call after many years. That so-called coincidence was God's grace that gave my father the chance to say goodbye to a good friend from our block in the Bronx.

WOODROW WILSON SMITH: THE LINGUIST

My father's most interesting friend to me and the one who introduced both my dad and me to the Spanish language was his good buddy Woodrow Wilson Smith, or "Smitty" as he was called.

Smitty was an inspiration to me for sure. And again, he and my dad encouraged me in the love of languages, particularly Spanish. Spanish, as I mentioned earlier, turned out to be one of the major tickets for balancing the karma I had with many souls.

"The Linguist" or "Smitty" was a language genius, and the dean of Languages at Bronx High School of Science for many years. He spoke many languages fluently, and he knew the dialects and pronunciation from their different regions—Spanish from Spain and from Costa Rica, French from Marseille and from Paris, German, Russian, Portuguese, Italian, Mandarin and Shanghai, and Russian.

My dad would invite me to go with Smitty and him to foreign restaurants. I loved these trips. At German restaurants, Smitty would speak flawless German, and the staff could not believe a black man could be so fluent. He would do the same at French restaurants, where he would entertain everyone for hours. There

I was, soaking all this up and loving it. Truth be told, Smitty had been in Army Intelligence and was one of the top German translators for our government during the Second World War. His language acquisition, he said, began while listening to the radio in North Carolina as a boy.

Smitty fascinated me. I believe he knew all of these languages from previous lifetimes. In fact, I believe Smitty had been a court interpreter for European kings. He was not only a linguist but also an intellectual and art connoisseur. He was truly amazing. With a cigarette almost always hanging from his lips, he would never finish his meal, for talking with everyone until the restaurant closed for the night. I believe he stepped right back into the world of languages in this life and became an example of excellence and genius in his field.

Smitty has since passed on.

ROMARE BEARDEN: THE ARTIST

I came from an experience of art and writing in previous incarnations. Romey was another friend of my father's who escorted me back to recollections of those times and a love of the world of art, literature, and politics.

I used to accompany my dad to Romey's loft in Greenwich Village in lower Manhattan. His home was filled with canvasses and the smell of paint. As a teen, I would listen to their conversations about his latest projects and tell him which of his works I liked the best. His wife would serve us tea.

Romare Bearden's artwork, now famous, is found in some of the major museums. He gave me a painting and one of his prints. When at his home, I felt myself immersed in a familiar environment of another time.

SUMMERS IN SAG HARBOR

My parents saved their money and built a modest house in Sag Harbor Hills, Sag Harbor, Long Island. I was about twelve years old. I helped my parents lay concrete and slab for the patio and plant trees in the front yard, later dedicated to my grandma and where they buried her ashes.

I had wonderful times there during the summers, spending all day at the beach swimming and hunting for clams and mussels in the creek with my cousin Wells. We would wander all day in the reeds in the creek, free as birds watching the sandpipers and catching blue crabs with our nets. Time seemed to stand still. Or was it that it went by so quickly? Before we knew it, it was time to call it a day and go home.

When I was older, my dad and I used to swim almost a mile out to the black buoy in Gardner Bay.

Sag Harbor was a child's paradise. Back in those days, the residents of Sag Harbors Hills were black, and everybody knew everybody. The roads were unpaved and sandy. In town, the most exciting thing for us kids was going to the one local movie theater. Every now and then, we would see Zsa Zsa Gabor, a famous actress, with a friend out for a movie night.

Kenneth, my husband, and our son Michael visited Sag Harbor Hills about seven years ago and it had changed quite a bit. Most of the people I knew back then were gone. The sandy roads were now black asphalt. In town, the simple five-and-dime stores and small local restaurants were gone too. Replacing them were trendy restaurants like *Bea Jones*, boutiques, coffee shops, and lots of tourists with lots of money.

As I matured into a young woman I went there less and less and only for short visits. My parents ultimately sold their house and moved to Florida to be in warmer weather. They were never afraid to change residences and move on from one place to another, even in their eighties and nineties. Every time they resettled, it was to a smaller place, and they had to decide what to take and what to leave behind.

LETTING GO

Their changing residences and having to let go of familiar places was a great lesson for me. I have learned that, on the spiritual path, you may find it necessary to move a great deal. I did. I was on a search, and it took me to various locales. This movement to new places and circumstances fostered agility and versatility of mind and heart. It required my letting go of familiar places and some old patterns of thinking and acting. As a result, the healthy aspects of my real self began to emerge.

For example, I had to learn to speak up for myself when I realized the price I was paying for not doing so. A case in point was when I spoke up about my supervisor teacher, I mentioned before, who lied to me about a change she needed to make in my evaluation. I told the principal. He agreed with me. After that, she felt uncomfortable in that school environment and so she left the next year. As a result of speaking up, I had no negative energy to bear in my soul that I would have had to bear if I had remained silent.

The consequence of feeling more worthy altered how I communicated with others. The responses were more appropriate, peaceful, and clear. In those moments, you could say that I had entered into a contract with my higher self that brought genuine dialogue to most encounters and no negative energy.

Of course, in some situations when I could have responded, it was better that I didn't. In those cases I learned to just quietly acknowledge to myself that this person is mistaken and move on.

Every situation is different. The point is this, just as we surrender the clothes that no longer fit us, we also learn to surrender the thoughts, emotions, and behaviors that no longer serve us. I see this happening when I observe my two selves side by side—the higher and the lower, "the little me" and "the big me" as the children are taught in some of their stories. I then have to make a choice—to go up or to go down.

The choice of the mystic is to identify with the divinely inspired thoughts, feelings, and actions—to try to go up. Paul the Apostle, in 1 Corinthians 15:31 said, "I die daily."

What is it that dies? You may ask.

It is the unreality of the "not self." It is all that is not Christ within me—my pride, my selfishness, my possessiveness, my vanity, my prejudice, and my fear. You name it; layer-by-layer, in the crucible of time, this substance is pushed up to the surface so I can choose to keep it or to let it go.

As I let go of the unreality of past thoughts and actions that lead nowhere but to grief and lock into the higher Realm, I see the world and people differently. I understand people as pilgrims in process, souls learning and growing, as I am, all of us making our way home. As I go higher up the ladder of initiation and testing, I see that I have more to let go of. A great deal of personal investment in others is withdrawn; my love and caring becomes less selfish, less needy. I am developing the sense that nothing really belongs to me, and in doing so, I have begun to experience a great liberation, a great freedom, not only for myself but also for those I love. I am allowing them to be themselves and not my idea of what they should be. Yet, I still keep in my heart a vision of them fulfilling their highest potential, their God potential.

My parents, in their nonattachment to places and familiar things were preparing me for the time I would leave to join the Summit Lighthouse in the 1980s. I packed up all I could get in my yellow Toyota station wagon, along with my two children, and, with great joy and anticipation, left all the rest behind.

My neighborhood in the Bronx, New York, Sag Harbor, learning foreign languages, my parents' world with their friends, my childhood friends, school—all supported me understanding myself. My home life and its advantages or disadvantages were what my soul needed to advance. My karma earned me my family and the society I grew up in with all of its opportunities. I came with a mission, and my parents ushered me along toward fulfilling that mission without them ever knowing it outwardly.

The law of karma and reincarnation has guided my journey through many lifetimes. It will continue to do so until I have paid all debts to others, balanced 51 percent of my karma, and fulfilled other requirements for the ascension,[23] the great goal of life for all of us. Then I will be home free.

Free to rest? Maybe for a while, but then to begin another adventure in the exploration of reality in the vast cosmos. Reality goes on forever. No boredom there.

What did my parents learn from me? My parents saw that I was a fiery, independent spirit and not afraid to follow my dreams. My determination and independence may have rekindled in them the memory and deep assurance of a path that leads to ultimate freedom in God and that it is for them as well. They loved me, and I pulled on those heartstrings in a way that maybe would not have happened without a "me" to care for. With the opening of their hearts they became, as all good parents, less selfish and self-centered. I brought them joy and, as well, sorrow. They worried about my independence and where I would eventually wind up.

They did not completely understand my spiritual quest. But my father, the philosopher, did understand it at a certain level, and I think he approved and was inspired. I taught him about the law of karma and reincarnation and that death is not final. This gave my father in particular a hope he did not have. Oh, he believed in the Great Spirit, but he thought everything would return to the earth as trees, sun, rain, and so on. He had a Christian upbringing too. His theology was a mixture of both.

When he lay dying in the hospital, I was called to his bedside

---

[23] "The future is what you make it, even as the present is what you made it. If you do not like it, God has provided a way for you to change it, and the way is through the acceptance of the currents of the ascension flame."

Serapis Bey and Annice Booth, "Introduction" in *The Path to Your Ascension* (Gardiner, Montana: SU Press, 1999), 38–45.

and was there to see him on. My husband told him to follow the Light. "Follow the light, Chuck. It will take you to higher realms."

My mom and dad were not particularly religious as I recall. They rarely went to church, except for funerals. They had gotten married in St. Phillips Episcopal Church in Manhattan, and the camp they were counselors at, Gilford Bower, was a church camp. My mother grew up as a Baptist. My parents lived honorable lives, and they never discouraged me from my beliefs, which as I have said, they often did not understand.

So you see, to be a mystic does not require having come from a deeply religious background. It may be a plus not to have. You don't then have to struggle with letting go of a particular indoctrination. I did not have any indoctrination to let go of, except that of Catholic school. The school kept me as an outsider and then finally rejected me when they told me I had to leave because of overcrowding. I was free to pursue truth as I found it. That truth revealed to me that I am a daughter of God and the divine resides within my heart. I can unite with this reality and master my environment in time. Finally and most beautifully, I can graduate from earth's schoolroom and become an ascended master. That is the path of the mystic—reunion with God, oneness with God, full integration with God.

When I had the epiphany experience in 1978 during the dictation by the master Kuthumi, it marked a turning point in my life. I seized the moment and pressed forward and have never turned back. It was during that experience that I determined to become a minister of Church Universal and Triumphant. [24] I am now a minister, and all that I know and am, and have experienced has helped me to help others. I am a better human being. I am actually more than that. I am increasingly a divine person, an integrated personality in God.

This is the difference between Christian orthodoxy and progressive revelation as taught by the ascended masters. The teaching is that we are to be like Christ, Christed ones, united as one with the second person of the Trinity, and follow in his footsteps—that he was not the exception but the magnificent example. He proclaimed that we could do likewise; he stated over and over again that it was the Father in Him that did the works and that he said nothing that did not come from the Father.

I know whatever good I do; it is God in me that does it. I do not profess to have accomplished the goal of reunion. I am a learner still and will always be a learner, even after I have ascended. For now, I have more to overcome and to let go of, but I am on my way!

An insightful realization that is presently bubbling up from my subconscious is the extent to which, in my youth, I went along with what other folks wanted me to do. It had to do with my lack of self-esteem and desire to please. Rather than pleasing God, I tried to please everyone else. This pattern goes

---

[24] Church Universal and Triumphant, founded in 1975, offers the seven sacraments of baptism, Holy Communion, confirmation, penance, marriage, anointing of the sick (including last rites), and ordination. These seven sacred rituals commemorate the seven rays of the Universal Christ.

See *The Teachings of the Ascended Masters* pamphlet, The Summit Lighthouse, 63 Summit Way, Gardiner, Montana 59030, www.summitlighthouse.org.

all the way back to the shame of being put out of the Garden of Eden, which is an allegory but also a part of cosmic history. I was there with my twin flame. We failed the test of obedience. That disobedience signaled the beginning of our separation from God and from each other. It made us feel ashamed and, yes, angry.

To this day, many of us retain the feeling of doubt and fear that our Father still loves us. We exclaim in our distress, "He is not really real." Or we cry out, "If he is real, it doesn't matter. I can do what I want. I'm in charge! He doesn't love me." We claim, "I don't need him!"

Thoughts and feelings like these remain in us, buried deep in our unconscious, and many of us would deny having them. When they come out, they are often disguised. The fear gives birth to anger toward God. "You did this to me. You threw me out of paradise. If you didn't want me to eat of the tree, why did you put it there in the first place?" And so on. Because we have difficulty in admitting we are angry with God, we project those feelings of anger onto our mothers or fathers, our husbands or wives, our children, or our political parties or social movements and other such outlets.

Or we are in a state of always trying to please everyone else but not God. This was reflected in my foolish and self-defeating behaviors in seeking the approval of others. I was saying, "Look, I'm worthy. I am a good person."

We clearly do not understand the profound consequences of our failing Lord Maitreya's initiation in the Garden of Eden. But God really understood it. Out of his love and mercy for us, He gave us messengers and angels as examples to teach us; and He wrote his law in our hearts. He also gave us, by the request of Saint Germain, the gift of the violet flame. And the chart of the I AM Presence which is a picture of our identity and pathway home.[25] We have all we need to pursue the pearl of great price.

---

[25] Saint Germain, hierarch of the Aquarian Age and sponsor of the United States of America, has given us the gift of the violet flame. The violet flame is a frequency of energy of the Holy Spirit that goes to the core of unreality and transmutes or changes the cause, effecting record and memory of it when invoked by us in the name of the Mighty I AM presences. Some of his past embodiments were Samuel the Prophet; Merlin the magician; Joseph, the father of Jesus, and Francis Bacon, writer of the Shakespearean plays.

Elizabeth Clare Prophet, *The Masters and Their Pretreats,* compiled by Annice Booth, (Gardiner, Montana: SU Press), 312–322.

5

College

I left New York for college in 1960, full of anticipation and a little anxious about what I would encounter. It was my first time really being away from home for an extended period. And you know how it is—new friends and new circumstances. Overall, academically I did okay. I really excelled in art and Spanish. I lived in a campus dormitory for the first year, Charles Gate Hall, from where I walked the seven blocks or so to class every day. The next three years until I graduated, I lived off campus in various places with friends.

Boston University was a huge school, one you could get lost in. My dad had wanted me to go to a small black college because his experience at Lincoln University had been so positive. He'd met some of his lifelong friends there, and he often spoke of the great camaraderie, social connections, and notable caring of the faculty for the students. I wanted the anonymity of a large university. It brought me some good experiences and some difficult karmic ones as well.

Spanish, art, ancient classical literature, world religions, and geology were my favorite subjects. They helped me to stay focused and engaged. The world religions professor inspired me, as he took on the persona of Buddha when he taught Buddhism. He was of Chinese origin and would come to class in saffron robes, be very peaceful, and talked slowly with deliberation. While teaching Confucianism, he would don the attitude of a wise teacher and also wear periodic clothing and so forth. The class reminded me of the many religious paths we may have followed.

I ask myself now, *What was it about these subjects that fascinated me so much?* I didn't know it then, but my soul must have tuned into something that enticed me to select them. It wasn't like I had to take them, except for one. Every one of those classes, as I look back now, offered reinforcement to my search toward understanding who I am.

Geology, the study of rock formations and crystals and the forces that shaped them must have made me inwardly question, what forces have shaped my inner and outer world? The subject matter of the course—stalactites and stalagmites; the precious stones; the purity of the white quartz; the immensity of some rock structures formed by pressure over time; and magnificent gems of all shapes, colors, and sizes invited me to consider the mystery of the outer and inner worlds and their beauty.

The study of world religions revealed how God had manifested himself differently throughout time and history to reach and teach diverse peoples and cultures. Studying the science of linguistics and the history and literature of the Spanish language, I was impressed by the almost infinite variety of word syllable combinations there are in the languages of the world. This beautiful, infinite variety and creativity is throughout creation. And I pondered it.

In terms of language, I have always believed you could never really know a culture if you didn't have some knowledge of its language or music. Both are keys that unlock the essence of a culture's uniqueness. For instance, in English we say, "How did you sleep last night?" In Spanish, people say, "How did you wake up with the morning?" Different ways of saying the same thing, but what a difference!

Studying the *Iliad* and *Odyssey* in Ancient Classical Lit took me to great battles of heroism and sacrifice. The story of Odysseus, the hero in the *Odyssey* by Homer, is all about the trials and tests on the path homeward.

My soul was searching, and some of the answers were right there in my classes at Boston University in the courses I was taking. My Holy Christ Self was showing me. If only I could have seen more clearly then.

I did find my first love while at Boston University. He was a writer, and I was smitten, really smitten. It was enthralling while it lasted. But like a firecracker, it burst with the most beautiful twinkling lights for a while, and then all the sparkle just faded— kaput! We parted as friends.

The challenging times I had in college were keeping up with difficult classes like statistics. I also had a few difficult karmic relationships to understand and untangle. These challenges, with both boyfriends and girlfriends, were softened and lightened by the study of the classes I was enrolled in.

It was in art especially, though, where, under the eye of my teacher, I put paint to canvas to my soul's content. The great masters whose work we copied—Delacroix, Tiepolo, Michelangelo—and my own personal creations took me back to the world of European art. I was there! Painting and drawing in my art class gave me the greatest satisfaction of all! My teacher displayed my work publically, and if my self-esteem had been low that day or week, painting and drawing compelled it out of the basement into the light.

Another satisfaction was playing bridge and pinochle in the student union between classes with my friends. Can't leave that out!

EUROPEAN ADVENTURE

In the summer of 1964 and after I graduated from BU, I went to Europe. A college friend and I had planned to go together. She was originally from Spain and had relatives who were flamenco dancers; that sounded intriguing. However, she backed out two weeks before we were to leave, presenting me with a decision to make. Should I not go? Find someone to go with me? Or should I go alone? I decided to go alone. I believe the confidence my parents had in me bolstered whatever confidence I had in myself.

When I arrived in Paris, I checked my bags into a locker on the Right Bank and took the metro to the Left Bank, pinching myself all the way to remember I was actually in Paris, France, by myself. All the stations were clearly marked, and I had no problem. The metro was beautiful and not marked up with black paint like the subways in New York. The streets and cafés were jam-packed with people chatting and laughing that day. I managed to find a café on the sidewalk that had some seats left and sat down; I ordered in the French I knew, a sandwich and a glass of wine. I needed to gather my thoughts and plan my next steps. It was a sunny day, and lots of people were on the sidewalks going about their business.

I was eating my sandwich when a young black man came up to me and asked, "Are you Bonnie Jones?"

A little shocked, I replied, "Yes I am."

He told me a friend of mine—one I knew from college and who had also been traveling in Europe—had told him to watch out for me. She had described what I looked like. Amazingly, he recognized me among all those people that day at that particular café. He also found me a place to stay.

I remained in Paris about a week and then took a train to Madrid, Spain, in hopes of finding a job and meeting up with the flamenco dancers.

Spain did not work out. I didn't find a job, and the dancers had their own "in" crowd, and I was not welcomed as a part of it. So much for that!

I returned to Paris by train that fall and reconnected with some people I knew. I was able this time, with the help of a Canadian friend, to get a job as a typist in a typing pool at an international organization. With that job, I was able to pay the rent on an apartment that I shared with some of my friends. It was on the Left Bank on Rue des Ecole near Sorbonne University. Every resident on our floor shared the same bathroom. We had to pay to use the shower.

Life in Paris in the mid-'60s was very different from what I was used to in the United States. The only supermarket in the entire city was on the swanky section of the Right Bank, which was expensive and far away. We had to make every thing from scratch. There were no boxes of cereal or pancakes or boxes of anything. I shopped every day at the open markets—where there were stalls for fruit, for dairy products, for bakery products, for vegetables, and for meat. Every type of food had its own stall. Because we had no refrigerator, which was common for some apartments then, we put our milk and butter on the windowsill. Shopping was fun, and I practiced my French with the merchants to my utter delight and to their chagrin! I loved living and working in Paris!

A year later, back in the United States of America, I worked for about a year at the United Nations in the Industrial Development Organization. Almost all the people I'd worked with in Paris came to work at the UN too—the Russian lady, the Czech gentleman, and the Canadian who found me the apartment in Paris. It was like old home week.

I had many wonderful experiences while living in Europe. There were two experiences that were outstanding. One was to be life changing and a foretelling of things to come on my spiritual path. The other was an opportunity to have an once-in-a-lifetime meeting with someone I greatly admired. I have to tell you. I felt such a freedom while traveling and working overseas. I wasn't married. I had no children and really no responsibility except to absorb the culture, practice my French, and to enjoy.

MAITREYA

The first life-changing experience in Paris was a vision I had of a golden clipper ship on a backdrop of a dark blue sea and sky. One bright, sunny day while walking down a cobblestone street from my apartment to the metro, I saw in my mind's eye a beautiful golden clipper ship. The memory of it kept repeating itself through the years. I was captivated by its beauty but had no idea what it meant.

It wasn't until many years later, when I became associated with the Summit Lighthouse, that I understood its significance. It was Maitreya's Mystery Ship crossing the sea of Samsara or illusion to enlightenment. Lord Maitreya[26] had come sailing into my life, informing me of something beautiful I did not yet understand. The vision was a foretelling of things to come spiritually. I would, in a future time, be pursuing the path to illumination. Lord Maitreya was the master in the Garden of Eden, and he had an invitation for me.

BROTHER MALCOLM X

The other experience I had was meeting Malcolm X.[27] He was on his way back from his hajj (the pilgrimage to Mecca every adult

---

[26] See previous footnotes on Lord Maitreya.

Lord Maitreya has come to the fore in this age to teach all who have departed from the Great Guru Sanat Kumara, from whose lineage both he and Gautama descended, and to bring again the opportunity for modern initiates to study in the mystery school from which we were removed, having failed the test of obedience.

On May 31, 1984, Jesus Christ announced in a dictation that Lord Maitreya was dedicating the Royal Teton Ranch as the place prepared for the reestablishment of his mystery school in this age. Jesus Crist, *The Mystery School of Lord Maitreya. May 31, 1984.*

Lord Maitreya is worshiped in Tibet, Mongolia, China, and Japan and throughout Asia as "the Compassionate One" and as the coming Buddha.

Maitreya maintains an etheric retreat over Tientsin, China, in the Himalayas, and at the Royal Teton Retreat in Montana.

To read more about Lord Maitreya, please see Mark L. Prophet and Elizabeth Prophet, *The Master and their Retreats* (SU Press: Montana, 2003), 202–2

Mark L. Prophet and Elizabeth Prophet, *The Master and their Retreats* (Montana: SU Press, 2003).

[27] Malcolm X, or as he was later known, el Hajj Malik el Shabazz, was a black nationalist leader of the Nation of Islam in the 1950s and '60s.

He broke with the organization and its leader, Elijah Mohammad, over doctrinal and personal policies. In the '60s, he made the holy pilgrimage to Mecca called the Hajj. There

Muslim is supposed to make at least once in his lifetime.) Some friends of ours were aware of his presence in the city and set up a meeting for all of us to talk with him.

When I was first introduced to him that afternoon, I was grinning from ear to ear. I couldn't believe I was actually meeting Malcolm X. He was tall and redheaded, just like his pictures.

Later that day, in a private meeting, we asked him questions about the issues of the day concerning black folk, the role of black women in society, what he would like to see in the future, and so forth. The discussion went on into the night, with us hanging on to every word. Those of us who spent this time with Brother Malcolm will always consider it very special. He was quite a charismatic figure and presented as someone very balanced, powerful yet peaceful, and insightful.

A French cinematographer made a hastily put together film of our meeting. For a period in the 1960s, it circulated among the Black Power movement[28] in New York. You could see Brother Malcolm and hear our questions and his answers. Our pictures were left out.

After he returned to the United States, we remained in Paris and formed an organization called Afro Americans in Paris. We

---

he had a life-changing spiritual experience that caused him to embrace all people, black and white, as brothers. It was then that he embraced traditional Islam.

El Hajj Malik el Shabazz was assassinated at the Audubon Ballroom in Harlem on February 21, 1965. He was thirty-nine years old. He left a wife and six children.

For further information, read Alex Haley *Autobiography of Malcolm X* (Shil Press: New York).

[28] The Black Power movement was a revolutionary movement that occurred in the 1960s and 1970s. It emphasized racial pride, economic empowerment, and the creation of political and cultural institutions.

invited Brother Malcolm back two or three months later, and this time we gave his visit a great deal of publicity. When he arrived at Orly Airport, the French police stopped him from entering the country. He returned to New York and was assassinated at the Audubon Ballroom in Harlem several months later. The year was 1965. We were devastated!

To have met Malcolm, el hajj el Malik Shabazz, and to have known him for that brief period in such a special way was an incredible experience for all of us. He was an example to me of a spiritual warrior who pursued truth, undeterred by what the consequences might be. I sensed he knew he was going to be assassinated; yet he spoke and lived what he believed. He must have been very concerned or even afraid, but he did not shirk from speaking his heart. His visit to Mecca had transformed him. He was not bitter toward whites; nor did he hate anyone. He wanted to heal the rifts between people and to help his beloved black brothers and sisters rise economically, socially, politically, and spiritually. I saw him fearlessly following the spiritual path wherever it would lead him. He was a powerful example to me.

Aside from the support of his wife and family and other believers, I would think, for him, it was a lonely path. For a while in Paris though, he could relax and enjoy the company and adulation of some young people who loved him.

Malcolm is back again. The Justice of reincarnation requires it. Khalil Gibran in his great book *The Prophet* says, "A little while, a moment of rest upon the wind and another woman shall bear me." I believe another woman has borne Malcolm X, and he is with us.

Traveling in Europe was wonderful! There with me was my guardian angel, my Holy Christ self guiding and protecting me for the future and giving me glimpses of it, like the beautiful ship of Lord Maitreya. I felt the freedom and excitement of a little child playing at the shoreline in Sag Harbor Hills, and I felt protected.

I returned to the United States, worked at the United Nations for about a year, and then enrolled in Hunter College to take courses in education to prepare for a career as a teacher. This was my dad's suggestion, and I followed it.

6

Identity

Who am I? I am a daughter of God, and I endeavor to identify with My Holy Christ self first and foremost. My Holy Christ self is the God self in me who is also the same God self in you. This is the meaning, metaphysically, of our "oneness." The outer me of race and sex are only the costume I wear for the drama of this present life. [29]

In my present life, I am black and female. I was born into a socially conscious, black, middle-class family. We lived in a black and Puerto Rican neighborhood, where I went to Catholic school with mostly kids like myself. I remember my one white friend,

---

[29] "Now I am well aware of the fact that down through the years men have stressed the differences of race and that the brown and the black have been questioned in particular. But if individuals will think of themselves as solar manifestations of the living God—recognizing that the outer garment of race that they wear is only an overcoat which they will one day put off—they will cease to think of themselves as white, black, yellow, red, or any other color. This attitude of mind is much to be desired, for while we cannot deny that racial prejudice does exist in the world—and that without our favor—we propose, as one of the first steps to the shedding of the racial consciousness, that men understand who and what they are. Man is not his body any more than he is his memory, his emotions, or his mind. He is a being. He has a body, he has a mind, he has a memory, and he has a spirit. The spirit of man is neither black nor white—it is forever free" (Beloved Chananda, Pearl of Wisdom 11, no. 30 [July 28, 1988]).

Go to www.summitlighthouse.org to sign up for Pearls of Wisdom.

Marianna Garibaldi. We all got along well. Later, I went to junior high and senior high school with mostly Jewish kids. I kind of stood out in that crowd.

HIGH SCHOOL

You could count the number of blacks in the school. My classmates called me by my nickname, Bonnie, and I remember one Jewish boy asking me, "Is your name really Bonnie Jones?" They were all Swartzes, Rubensteins, and Cohens. We had a football team with cheerleaders, and I was the only black cheerleader, the token. I really didn't fit in culturally. Many of the senior girls were looking forward to marriage and having families after high school. That was far, far from my mind. I was headed to college. It was expected, and the other girl of color and I used to shake our heads and ask ourselves, Four more years, can de do four more years of school? Ugh!

However, most of the students were congenial and I experienced no prejudice from them. In fact, some of them were pretty friendly. I had a Jewish friend who invited me to her home several times. It was just that my Jewish friends like the flamenco dancers in Spain, had their own "in" groups, and the very few black students at the school were not a part of them.

The school was William Howard Taft up on the Grand Concourse. It is now all black, all of the Jews having moved to Brooklyn or Long Island years ago.

JACK AND JILL

As a teen, I was invited to be a member of Jack and Jill, a black middle-class social network. In the membership were future lawyers and judges and Ronnie Brown, a future secretary of commerce under President Bill Clinton. Friends in the group had relatives who were the first leaders in their fields—first black Manhattan borough president, Edward Dudley; first black fire chief, Wesley Williams; first black ambassador to the United Nations, Ralph Bunch. We were all shades of brown and tan. I fit in.

MY VIEW OF PEOPLES AND CULTURES

Being black was obviously a very important part of my growing up experience. I've learned that race in itself is an outer symbol that small-minded people use to put you in a box.

Race, all by itself, may seem to be the basis of some exclusion or rejection. But that rejection among blacks can also have to do with culture—the Northerner versus the Southerner, the West Indian versus the American black, and the Hutu versus the Tutsi.

And sometimes it's just karma, either personal karma or group karma. You don't like someone or they you because you have some karma to balance together. This goes for groups also, some Arabs with some Jews for instance, some blacks and some whites.

I have found that the resolution to this conundrum comes with a change of heart. As I began to recognize God in myself as a reality with whom I could have a direct relationship, I began to be able to acknowledge that same God in other people. As a result, I realized my neighbor is just like me in many respects, grappling with the joys and challenges of living. We all want the same things after all—happiness; freedom from fear, poverty, and loneliness; and, most of all, we all want love. As my love of God intensified, my capacity to love other people expanded. As I get glimpses of the unfolding of God's design in myself and in my friends, coworkers, and family members, I am less critical, less judgmental, more loving, and more in awe.

My view of peoples and cultures was broad, and I did appreciate the variety. Not everybody I met had that same appreciation. My father used to take my friends and me to house parties someone in our little group of friends had been invited to. One particular night, he took me to a party in Brooklyn, and I was by myself. He walked me up to the door and told me he would pick me up when I called. I went in and immediately I saw this group of black folk did not welcome me.

Everyone in the room was stuck on what I looked like and could not see me. It was my skin color. My skin tone was just too light. The folks there gave me a stare that told me so. I could get rejection like this from both blacks and whites. I was either too light or not black enough for some of my own. Or I was called "high yellow," a term I despised, by some whites. You see, I was a reminder to some Southern white women and Northern ones too of the mischief of their men during slavery and beyond.

I called my dad, and he came and got me. I had awhile to wait before he got there, and it was very uncomfortable. I felt deep rejection.

Rejection is painful. There are reasons for rejection that sometimes have nothing to do with you or me as a person and everything to do with what you or I represent. In this case in Brooklyn, I'm not sure what I represented, maybe a privileged person, a snob, or someone who felt superior. Who knows? Sometimes it's economic status or place of birth that's the hated symbol. What we don't know we fear and then hate. I didn't go to any more parties in Brooklyn.

A "Brother" Who Knew His Goal

We see this prejudice everywhere and with many people, and it is very unfortunate. I remember an African friend of mine from the Congo. He came to Maryland and got a job in a restaurant washing dishes. He was the only black and was ostracized by the other kitchen employees. He had a tremendous attitude and work ethic. In spite of his coworkers' behavior toward him, which was deplorable, he was congenial. He had a goal and was focused on that.

When his coworkers got to know him, they started to like him. He was a good worker and willing to fill in for any of them when they were late or could not work. Because they got to know him, he was no longer a symbol but a person. They all became friends, and he, in a short time, achieved his short-term goal and became the headwaiter. And that was only the beginning for him.

Immersed In "Blackness," For Awhile

I mention my African friend because Africa and Africans were to play a part in my journey later on. Sometime after enrolling in Hunter College, in the '60s, I married a man from Guinea, West

Africa. He was the son of an imam who had made the Hajj. My husband himself was not a religious Muslim.

The marriage did not last, but it was during that time that I was caught up in the "Black Power" movement. Rap Brown, Stokely Carmichael, Angela Davis, Malcolm X, and others were my heroes. They had a mission, and that idea of a mission really appealed to me, as did belonging to what had the status of an "in group." In those days, I wore dashikis and long African dresses and a wrap around my head. I even had a small dashiki business with a friend from Brooklyn. I was a part of that crowd for a spell. It was fun wearing the pretty African clothes. The fascination soon faded for me, and so did the prominence of the movement. I still love those dresses and I wear them even today from time to time.

I know many blacks have had terrible encounters with whites. I didn't. Because I was mistaken for a Latina or Portuguese, I didn't experience the hard-core racial rebuffs that others received. My experiences were generally subtler—a few condescending teachers, some hard stares, an inappropriate accusation of something my children or I were supposed to have done and didn't. We had a clerk follow us around in a store suspicious we were shoplifting.

But there was one occurrence of racial name-calling I did experience in Richmond, Virginia, in the '70s that hurt. I was walking down the street when a white woman yelled out of her window, "High yella," and, "Get out of my front yard."

I had never been called that before. I had never even heard of the term. Her words were sharp and angry, and they stung.

Aside from that, I never experienced persistent, pervasive

racial hatred or discrimination that I was aware of. I grew up in the Bronx, New York, where there were no "black" and "white" water fountains and bathrooms.

RACIAL PREJUDICE

Racial prejudice is ignorance. We are more than just our bodies. We are spiritual beings with a soul that uses a body—black, white, yellow, or red, male or female—to experience life and put on more of our Christhood. If you are white now, you could have been black or any race in previous incarnations and vice versa. When I really got it, that the "I AM" in me is God in me, I was free and could see people's prejudices for what they were— ignorance of their true nature. That comment, "high yellow" would not bother me so much now—only the fact that the woman in the window was so hateful. I know her soul must be suffering and longing for true liberation. She's a pitiful creature actually.

That liberation comes through love. What hurt me the most and cut the deepest as a mother was whenever my children were mistreated, when they were ignored or put down by teachers or others. It wasn't always racial prejudice, but it happened when adults were insensitive, fanatical, and didn't understand the fragility of a child.

I forgive them. It's hard, but I do forgive them! No doubt, as a teacher, I have done the same to some child in ignorance.

Viewing people as "souls" rather than people, souls who have come into incarnation many times to learn the lessons of life, has given me a truer view of all of us. It has softened any criticism or rejection I might have of others or of myself.

THE SENSITIVITY OF BLACK FOLK

I think most black folks have great sensitivity. We identify with the downtrodden, as we have been the downtrodden, and some still are. We are willing to extend a hand, and we have forgiving hearts. We have suffered so much through slavery and it effects up to the present that many of us have wisdom and compassion for others who may also be suffering—virtues of mercy and a keen sense of justice.

I needed to have this sensitivity reintroduced and reinforced in me. I am a daughter of Afra, one who is pointing others of our kind toward the goal of life, the ascension. And so I needed a colored body and a black cultural environment to fulfill my role. This and the Latino communities have given me the mutual opportunity to balance karma.

I also believe black people, because of their compassion and capacity for forgiveness, are natural "servants" in the highest sense of the word. To be a servant is a powerful thing. It is the opposite of being a victim. It is to be like Christ.

Every person is a gem. We all have our divine blueprints. Being black is a part of my physical/cultural blueprint that I have embraced with love and great joy. Races are rays from the great causal body of God and all races have their gifts to give. Light bearers of whatever race are of the "I AM race"—all of us! We are all vital to the fulfillment of the majestic tapestry God has envisioned—a tapestry of purity, beauty, harmony, love, faith, and freedom essential to complete His grand design for this planet.

I am a daughter of Afra. That means I am of the blue and violet ray or race with the spiritual mandate to externalize the virtues of those rays—faith, honor, freedom, justice, and forgiveness. Inwardly I knew this. Now I had to find the others.

Finding My Spiritual Community

I started searching for answers to the mysteries of life when I graduated from college. After I came back from Europe, I began looking for that community of souls I was a part of—my mandala, my group that I knew in my heart existed somewhere. I used to go down to Second Avenue in New York and chant with the Hare Krishna folks. I read Paramahansa Yogananda's, *The Autobiography of a Yogi* and believed every word of it to be true. Yogananda, an Indian yogi and founder of the Self-Realization Fellowship, introduced the concept of guru to me and millions of people in the West. After reading his book, I went looking for my teacher.

LOOPS OF LIFE

I returned to Boston in 1970, where I got a fellowship for my master's degree in education at BU. It was there that I met Sandy and Michael. They were looking for a spiritual path too, and so we looked together.

I was desperate to find God. I was going through a difficult relationship and, rather than choosing the psychology approach to solving my anguish, I turned to God. I found an Eastern discipline that, ultimately, was not for me. But it did help me to get through my crisis.

I kept on searching. It's funny, though, how life loops around. At the time of that search, we found the teachings of Sri Aurobindo and the Mother. The discipline was called Supramental Yoga and was taught to us by a very kind man by the name of Mickey Flynn. Many years later, a friend, who was a salesman for some of the Aurobindo books, gave my husband and me a stack of brand-new books, about twenty of them, to store for him.

My present husband, Kenneth and I, kept those books in our attic for over fifteen years. A few years ago we decided to dispose of them, as we had not heard from our friend in many years. They were beautifully bound books, and I did not want to just throw them out or take them to the local library. So I investigated and found an Aurobindo retreat in New York State. I called the proprietors and asked if they wanted these books. Of course they did want them.

We started talking, and I mentioned that, years ago in Boston, I'd had a teacher, a very nice man named Mickey Flynn. Well, it turned out that they knew him well. He had died, and they had spread his ashes on their land.

A life loop I call it. Those are experiences or objects or places that come full circle for closure. Another example is when I passed the house we are now living in and the school where I used to teach many times, never realizing that we would live there or that I would be teaching there someday. I took special notice of the house and the school and had an intuitive recognition of them each time I passed.

Loops of life—have you experienced loops like these?

FINDING THE BOOK THAT OPENED THE DOOR

Life moved on, time passed, and now I was married with two beautiful children. I worked as director of the Reading and Study Skills center at Virginia Union University and, later, at Virginia Commonwealth University in Richmond, Virginia. Not too far from Virginia Union, I found what my soul was looking for. I was thirty-five years old, and it was fifteen years after beginning my search.

While browsing through a new age bookstore, I picked up a book from the shelf entitled *Studies of the Human Aura*. It contained dictations by the master Kuthumi Lal Singh transcribed by Elizabeth Clare Prophet. Kuthumi, as I mentioned earlier, was Saint Francis of Assisi in another incarnation. I knew I had found gold at the end of the rainbow when I read his words in that book. It was as if the master were speaking directly to me.

Not long after that, I prepared to leave Richmond for a conference in Pasadena, California, where I had the epiphany experience—the experience of the indwelling Christ. Inside the book was a description of hierarchy, the idea that all creation springs from the Divine Light, the Mighty I AM presence, and Elohim and to lesser forms of God manifestations— archangels, Christed-ones, angels, and nature spirits. This heavenly hierarchy has a name. It is called The Great White Brotherhood. I understood that heaven was real, complex, and beautiful.

Moving To Malibu

I had already attended two conferences, so by then I knew a few people. I had also attended a three-month intensive at Summit University, after which I was invited to join staff. Most of the students were given assignments, either at the California headquarters or at teaching centers throughout the world. I did not make the decision immediately. It was a huge decision. But nothing was working out in Richmond, and all arrows were pointed toward a new life, a new location.

It wasn't long after that, that I re-arranged my life and quit my job. I left Richmond for the Summit Lighthouse headquarters in California in my yellow Toyota station wagon with my two children and all of the possessions I could carry. I had little knowledge of what my life would be like once there. I had been invited to join the Summit Lighthouse staff, and my children were promised free admission to the Summit's Montessori school. My father joined us in Nashville, Tennessee, to help with the drive.

The Tests Begin

When we arrived, the tests began. The staff member who'd made the arrangement for my volunteering was not there. No one had heard of me, and no one knew about my agreement to teach in exchange for schooling for my children. I was told the school staff were at a conference and would be back, but no one was sure when.

Meanwhile, public school was to start in a week, and I felt duty bound to get my children registered. We also needed a place to live. My father did not know what to think either. But he figured I had made my bed, and now I had to sleep in it. He had met a few of my friends, and so he knew I would find lodging with them and not be homeless. He took a flight back to New York the next day.

That same day in Summit's cafeteria, I met a woman who lived in Agora Hills with her son and some other members of the organization. She told me she had a place for us to stay. I asked her how she had known I needed a place. She said God had told her.

I looked at her in amazement. "God has told you?" I asked.

"Yes," she said.

I knew in my heart God would take care of me. He had taken care of me all my life and all through Europe. Why would I doubt that he would take care of me now? Oh ye of little faith! Speaking of myself that is.

I enrolled my children in a public school and was settling in to the notion that plans may have changed regarding my position as teacher at the Summit's Montessori school. I was disappointed but ready to move on.

A week later, the Montessori staff returned and a staff member, who was told where I was staying, called me and asked if I was ready to volunteer and enroll my children. Being relatively settled in my new situation, with my children enrolled and ready to go to school in a few days, I had to rethink whether or not I now wanted to volunteer. She gave me twenty-four hours to make up my mind.

The next morning, I came to her office and said yes. It was what I really wanted to do, although I was smarting a bit, having been left in limbo for a period. *Oh ye of little faith*, I thought again of myself.

Those are the kinds of tests you encounter on the path. I

had to reassert my desire to follow the teacher whatever the obstacle. Reaffirmations of my right and desire to be on the path periodically came up in large and small ways. In this case, it was an exercise of free will without coercion or persuasion, but with a boundary—a simple question posed. "What do you want to do?" And an answer, in this case, was required in twenty-four hours.

Free will is paramount with the masters. God does not force us to do anything. That is also the case of the "true" teacher.

I had made up my mind, and the next day I enrolled my children in the Summit's Montessori school and began volunteering. Of course, my own faith or lack of it I duly noted.

FINDING WORK

All that I left—the security of a good job, housing, and friends—I have never regretted. Nor has my present husband. But right then, I was faced with the reality of having to find work to help pay rent and to buy food!

Because I volunteered during the day, I found evening jobs, and they were varied and interesting. I worked packing meat in a supermarket until I told my supervisors, in my exuberance, that it was not honest for them to pack the fat on the bottom so that people wouldn't see it. I had that job for about a week. I worked as a guard at the Marguardt Corporation, an aeronautical and engineering firm in Van Nuys that help build space shuttles. Mostly, I worked teaching English as a second language at Reseda Community Adult School, Evans Community Adult

School, Pepperdine University, and a church in China Town, Los Angeles.

In between all of that, I sold crystal jewelry from time to time for a member of our group who had kiosks in the various department stores in the area. Plus, I tutored a Brazilian lady in English. I was busy, busy! And it was great!

Of course, I attended services, and every Sunday there were two or three dictations from the ascended masters about what was happening on the planet, our role, God's will and the path of personal Christhood. It was beyond fabulous to be able to sit at the feet of the masters and to hear the sermons and seminars from Elizabeth Clare Prophet.

MY CHILDREN

I took my first two children, from a previous marriage, Spirit and
Sumner with me to California when I left Richmond. They loved
living with other families and children in Agora Hills Canoga
Park and other places. They attended the church's Montessori
school and had fun participating in activities with their friends.
Everything was an adventure.

Later, when Kenneth and I were directors of the Los Angeles
Teaching Center, they lived with us on that property. As far as
I know, they were the only children who have ever lived there.
They delighted in hiding behind bushes, playing hide-and-seek
and other games. The property was beautiful, and there were lots
of places to hide.

When I was a young woman, I never dreamed of having children. The test came upon me unexpectedly. Evidently, like marriage, I needed to be a parent for the rounding out of my experience. Not all women or men need to be parents. Many have already played that role in previous lifetimes, and that was sufficient. But here I was at twenty-nine, not in the best of circumstances, and pregnant with my first, a girl—Spirit Ananda Augusta. I was joyous to be pregnant with her.

While she was in my womb, I was engrossed in reading spiritual literature. One day as I lay on the couch reading the *Bhagavad Gita* about Krishna and Arjuna in the Battle of Kurukshetra, her soul began communicating to me how much she wanted to be born and how much she loved what I was reading.[30]

So I made a point each day to lay down somewhere quiet and read aloud to her soul. She was three months in my womb at this time. We had a wonderful soul communication up until the time she was born. This may seem really strange to some of you. But you know, if you get quiet enough for a long enough period, you may hear the whispers of angels and even the voice of God. I was in a very peaceful location, and I had no responsibilities, thanks to a dear friend. So I was receptive.

My son Sumner Charles Colson Madden came three years after Spirit. He had a "damn-the-torpedoes" personality and has

---

[30] Krishna and Arjuna are protagonists in the great battle drama of Kurukshetra, which is described in the Hindu text the *Bhagavad Gita*.

Krishna, the divine personality, disguises himself and is Arjuna's charioteer in the battle. In the midst of the battle, Arjuna becomes dejected and unable to continue as he views some of his friends and relatives on the opposite side. He refuses to fight, upon which Krishna reveals himself and expounds on the nature of the soul and the meaning of dharma or duty. Krishna then as guru and Arjuna as disciple is reassured that it is his duty to fight and, moreover, that the soul cannot be killed (Krishna.org, www.opposingviews.com).

always been fearless and sometimes reckless. This caused me to worry a lot. One time, he jumped into a pool when he was just two and could not swim. Of course we rescued him, and the experience didn't seem to faze him a bit. Other times, he ran down hills at top speed with abandon, rode his bike the same way, and played in the streets of Agora Hills where tarantula spiders roamed. Needless to say, he acquired a few knots on his head and bruises on his body.

One day, on my lunch hour, I went to Sumner's classroom. He was entirely absorbed in some Montessori material, to the point that he didn't even notice me standing right by him. I was literally there for about ten minutes observing him before he finally looked up. When he did, the expression on his face was far, far away, and he looked as if he had just seen something quite miraculous.[31]

Sumner, the rambunctious child, is the most settled of my children now. He is married with three beautiful and talented children, Isaac, Laila, and Elise; a supportive wife; and a job he loves.

Spirit and Sumner graduated from Hampton University in Virginia.

Michael Justice Excalibur Frazier is my youngest child, and Kenneth, my husband, is his father. Kenneth and I were on the spiritual path before Michael was conceived. He is definitely a recently reincarnated soul, and it is justice that he is here today with us.

Michael was born right after we took a bus trip back from Savannah, Georgia. We had just attended a Montessori

---

[31] The true teachings and methods of Maria Montessori link the child to his inner teacher. See http://www.Age of Montessori.org.

information course presented by Madame Caspari, a protégé of Maria Montessori.[32] The bus arrived at 5:00 p.m.; I registered my two older children for school and then went straight to the hospital, where Michael was born at 8:03 p.m. What a day!

Michael is independent of thought and speaks his mind quite fearlessly. He has a huge heart. He loves animals and plants and books, especially history books. He'd make a great history teacher. Like many millennials right now, he's making ends meet in a so-so job. In his early years in Montana, Michael got involved with scouting and followed through with it when we moved to Maryland. He later became an Eagle Scout.

Michael is a graduate of the University of Maryland.

I love my children dearly. When I take an inventory as to how successful I think they are, I don't simply look at externals. I look to see if they are overcomers of obstacles, negative peer pressure, and attraction to the drug culture. Are they selfish, insensitive? What virtues are they externalizing? They all have been exposed to the teachings of the ascended masters. Now they have to choose whether or not they will follow those teachings. I don't know who said this, but it seems true and wise. "God has no grandchildren." I interpret this to mean that each of us has to come to God in our own way and in our own time and not by our parents.

---

[32] Madame Caspari was a member of our spiritual community and trained many teachers in the Montessori method as taught by her friend and teacher Maria Montessori. Mary Ellen Maunz, program director for *The Age of Montessori*, a teacher-training program embodying the authentic teachings of Maria Montessori, travels worldwide bringing these principles to others.

Maria Montessori, *The Absorbent Mind*, (AMI – Association Montessori Internatioanale (The Montessori Series Book) June 6, 2019

Maria Montessori, *The Secret of Childhood:* (Ballantine Books, NY, NY)

ABORTION IN A NEW LIGHT

It is hard work yet it is a blessing to have a child, a blessing for the parent and for the child. As mothers and fathers, we sponsor a soul's opportunity to fulfill her mission. Both parents then gain merits of good deeds for doing that. And of course the gift to the child is life and the opportunity to complete or carry on with her purpose. This gives abortion new meaning, doesn't it? When a child is aborted, it is the abortion also of that child's ability to fulfill a desire, a mission, which she may have been working on for ages. If we are made in the image of God, and we are, then abortion is also the murder of God in the womb.

The masters say that having an abortion does not prohibit us from making our ascension in this life, as long as we are repentant, never do it again, and serve life and children in some way. We all have made mistakes and God forgives us when we are penitent.

Every soul comes with a promise of fulfillment, as I have said throughout these memoirs. Each soul is on a journey homeward, and each incarnation offers new steps; new challenges; new experiences; new ways to master what must be mastered; and, perhaps, a final completion of something. We, as parents or caregivers, do not always know necessarily what our children's mission is or what their challenges will be. We try to prepare them to be resilient. We sacrifice to give them what we think they need; we try to get them ready for whatever they may face. Sometimes we do it poorly. I don't think I did it so well in every case. I look back and see things I could have done, should have done. You know how that goes if you are a parent—all of the "should haves" and "could haves." I found I had to forgive myself of those things and move on.

My children have their challenges too, as all of us in this world do. They are strivers, and they're resilient. And so I see them overcoming those challenges in time.

Having children required that I expand my heart. My children continue to teach me humility, patience, forgiveness, and how to let go.

8

Encounters with Angels
and the Messenger
Elizabeth Clare Prophet

C amelot and the Teaching Center and Ashram of the World Mother in Los Angeles were magical places. Before I made the decision to move there to become a staff volunteer, I had an experience with the messenger that, for me, was very significant.

In The Garden

I had already had my epiphany experience. And now, a year later, I was at my second conference. The conference was just over, and people had gathered for a reception at the Ashram of the World Mother, one of our retreat homes. The ashram was just off Arlington and Wilshire Boulevards.

I was there with a friend. We were told we would have an opportunity to meet Mrs. Prophet at the reception on the lawn. So off we went! It was a beautiful, bright sunny day, and she and many conferees were in the garden. I tried to get near her. But there were always two or three people talking with her. I did get close enough to brush up against her clothing. Funny, I don't actually remember what she was wearing that day, the color of her clothes, or anything about them. I do remember that she took notice of me having touched her.

My friend and I never got the chance to talk with her. At about 9:00 p.m., we said our goodbyes, and I called my cousin Wells, who lived near by, to pick me up. While I was sitting on the curb waiting for him, I had a beautiful experience of the messenger's presence with me. My desire had been fulfilled because, in this marvelous encounter, all the questions I was going to ask her had been answered.

Much later, as I thought about it, it reminded me of a biblical passage: "And behold, a woman that was diseased with an issue of blood twelve years came behind Him and touched the hem of his garment. For she said within herself, if I may but touch his garment, I shall be whole. But Jesus turned him about, and when he saw her, he said, Daughter, be of good cheer; thy faith hath made thee whole" (Matt 9:18–26 KJV).

I wondered what that experience meant for me personally. Cycles often come in groups of twelve years. I have experienced this in my life.

I interpreted the reference "an issue of blood" as referring to light. Blood is symbolical of light and the Christ consciousness in mystical terms.[33] I asked myself a question: Had I been in situations these last twelve years where I was losing my light, the spiritual fire I had gained?

I was still stuck in a negative relationship. Could it be that? I asked myself.

I came to the conclusion that I'd been losing ground in the relationship I was in, and I knew ending it was critical. It wasn't until I had the experience of my own personal Christhood that all of this became clear. Now, with this experience with the messenger, I knew where I belonged and that this was the spiritual community I had been searching for all this time. I wasn't dramatically made whole, like the woman with the issue of blood; but something really beautiful had happened. I had found

---

[33] "Therefore the plea for freedom is the plea to enter into the ritual of the use of the Ruby Ray. For it is the light of the blood, the light of the rose cross, that flows from the heart of the Christed- One who is in the very act of sacrifice unto the Lord" (Beloved Lord Ling, *Pearl of Wisdom* 24, no. 4, "The Class of the Archangels" [January 1981]). See https://summitlighthouse .org for *Pearls of Wisdom*.

the community I was looking for and I had been cut free from the emotional attachment to my negative situation. So I had actually been healed of a harmful state of mind.,

This community of the Holy Spirit had gone through quite a bit of negative publicity. We had been called a cult and had our members accused of being brain washed. Families of some of our members had called deprogrammers, and old members for various reasons had brought us to trial.

Yet I have never doubted the reality of these teachings or the integrity of the messenger. I was bonded forever to her in deep affection and love.

My friends used to say, speaking of me, "Oh she's going through a phase. Just wait a few months or years. She'll be on to something else."

Not so! This experience was early in my association with the messenger, but it would be to me the confirmation that kept me keeping on these forty plus years.

ARCHANGEL MICHAEL

Since that experience, I would communicate with Mother from time to time and see her different places on the campus, in the classroom, and at festivities. When I entered ministerial training, I also got firsthand instruction from her.

Another miraculous encounter, experienced not just by me but my many of us, took place on the campus at Camelot. Camelot, headquarters of the Summit Lighthouse and Church Universal and Triumphant, was a truly miraculous place, so full of angels. You could just think of someone you needed to see and they would be in front of you in a wink.

One night, after a dictation by Archangel Michael,[34] many chelas (disciples) were gathered with Mother on the patio next to El Morya's room at Camelot.[35] AV began playing Archangel Michael's "Victory March". Just then, swirls of blue lightning and electric blue fire spiraled into the patio.

Everyone's mouth flew open, and there were cheers of "Hail Archangel Michael! Hail Archangel Michael!"

Archangel Michael, cited in Revelation, is the one God chose to cast out the fallen angels from heaven. He is also the great protector of the woman and her seed. We are her seed, the sons and daughters and children of God, and he is our great protector who we call on often. There are many stories people tell in our community about how they were helped by Archangel Michael. Just about everybody has an Archangel Michael story.

Mother was there, of course, she had to be for it to happen. It was another one of those many displays of God's playfulness.

Sometimes, after dictations, there were symbols in the sky representing a master. Once, after a dictation by Mighty Astrea, feminine Elohim of the First Ray of God's Power, Astrea's circle

---

[34] Archangel Michael is known as Defender of the Faith, Champion of the Woman and her Seed, and Leader in the Battle of Armageddon. He stands as the defender of Christ consciousness in in all children of God. He is the greatest and most revered angel in Jewish, Christian, and the Islamic scriptures and traditions.

Mark L. Prophet and Elizabeth C. Prophet, *Saint Germain on Alchemy: Formulas for Self-Transformation* (Gardiner, Montana: Summit University Press, 1993), glossary.

[35] El Morya is founder of the Summit Lighthouse and the guru and teacher of the messengers Mark L. Prophet and Elizabeth Clare Prophet, Mark L. Prophet and Elizabeth Clare Prophet, *The Masters and their Retreats Compiled and edited by Annce Booth* (Gardiner, Montana: Summit University Press, 2003) 87-92

and sword were plainly visible to everyone in the sky above the chapel.

The castle of King Arthur and the Knights of the Round Table came alive and lived again at Camelot in Malibu, California, where all pursued the search for the Holy Grail, the "indwelling Christ."

The church moved from California and Camelot to Montana in the mid-eighties. The Inner Retreat at the Royal Teton Ranch where it is located is called the place of great encounters. There too people have stories of seeing the masters and elemental life.[36] God is real, and his kingdom is real!

BONITA, DON'T FORGET TO EAT YOUR DAIKON!

I was an elder of the church and in Montana for elder business when Mother's secretary called to invite me to join Mother and a guest from Africa for dinner. I gladly accepted, and later that evening, I went down to the ranch, through the gate, and on to her home. It was a modest home with certain upgrades befitting her station.

The guest was there when I arrived. I believe he was from Uganda. We had a meticulously prepared macrobiotic meal, and daikon radish was served as a part of the meal. The daikon is a white radish that helps with digestion and the assimilation of fats. During the meal, Mother told me, "Bonita, don't forget to eat your daikon."

---

[36] Elemental beings of fire, air, water, and earth are servants of the physical plane and act as the platform for the soul's evolution. Fire elementals are called salamanders, water elementals are undines, and earth elementals are gnomes.

Mark Prophet and Elizabeth Clare Prophet, *Saint Germain on Alchemy* (Montana: Summit University Press, 1993), glossary.

Afterward, we had a nice discussion about world events. Mother bought me a stack of dictations from the masters we call *Pearls of Wisdom* and invited me to sit in the rocker and enjoy myself while she shared some private time with her guest. Afterward, when it was time to leave, she asked me if I would give her guest a ride to his hotel in Gardiner. I was more than happy to do so.

When I arrived at the gate of her property, it was locked, and I did not have a key. I drove back to her home and knocked on the door. She opened it, and I told her the gate was locked. She then instructed her assistant to open it for me, and she again reminded me, "Bonita, eat your daikon!"

She never told me why, and for some reason, I did not ask. However, I obviously needed to eat daikon for my health, and she saw that.

Now this was very interesting to me because I fully understood later that the teacher would go to any lengths, even a locked gate, to make sure I took seriously a personal message and an expression of concern for my health. "Bonita, eat your daikon!"

I have shared this story with fellow disciples of the ascended masters during a tribute to Mother after her passing on October 15, 2009.

An Earlier Contact With An Angel Before I Met The Messenger

Some time before I moved to Montana with my children, we moved into a very nice house in Henrico country, Virginia. We had just moved in and a telephone man had come to fix the wires for our new phone. He never rang the bell but just went outside to do his work. He was outside doing what was needed to connect the new phone and the children were watching. He gently and affectionately patted each one and continued his work without looking up. I was watching him too. When he finished, he turned and I was able to see his eyes. They were brilliant like diamonds so that you could not see his face. He never said a word and just waved and left. I was astounded. I had never seen eyes like that. They were like two mini suns.

> *Be not forgetful to entertain strangers: for thereby*
> *some have entertained angels unawares.*
>
> Hebrews 13:2 KJV

9

The Dharma

Dharma literally means, "carrying," "holding" that which holds one's true nature. An individual's dharma is his duty to fulfill his reason for being. It is his divine plan that runs as a thread through all his lifetimes. When one's dharma is fulfilled, one's Three-Fold Flame balanced and sufficient karma is redeemed, the soul is eligible for the Ascension, the permanent bonding to God.
—ECP, The Buddhic Essence: Ten Stages to Becoming a
Buddha (SU Press, 2009) and ECP, The Path to Your
Ascension: Rediscovering Life's Purpose (SU Press)

Your dharma is your life's work, the work into which you infuse the God virtues you are acquiring. It is your blueprint or divine plan, your duty to life that carries you toward your ascension.

My dharma is teaching and preaching with the spoken and written word. Preparation for it in this life began after I finished completing my teacher certificate at Hunter College in New York in 1966 and continued with the epiphany in 1978, joining staff as a volunteer, and meeting and marrying my husband. Developing the art of Teaching Spanish helped me to accelerate on the path, showing me what I needed to hone as virtues and what I needed to give up to be able to enter the next phase of my journey.

We are now living in Silver Spring, Maryland. What follows is the story.

I BEGIN TEACHING

The first job I had as a teacher was at an Intermediate School in the Bronx. It was 1966. I taught social studies, art, and physical education in Spanish. The school needed someone to teach those subjects in Spanish, and I leaped at the opportunity. I was a new teacher, fresh and idealistic.

After that experience, life must have had a different plan for me because, for years, I taught everything but Spanish. I taught English as a second language to Chinese-speaking, Vietnamese, and Thai people in Los Angeles and to very sweet South American people who, more than anything, wanted to learn English. I never had any challenges or difficulties in these jobs, and I believe I was able to make some good karma with the students.

The rubber met the road when I actually started teaching high school Spanish in Maryland. I was fifteen years into my teaching career when this happened. I used to have a recurring dream that I was teaching in a hall of learning. I would pass by a room where the door was always closed but full of students. I knew I was supposed to be in there teaching, yet I avoided that room like the plague. For many years, I avoided it. When I finally began teaching, I understood what the dream had meant and why I had avoided that room.

A Trial By Fire:[37] The Proving Ground

It was culture shock when I began teaching in Maryland. I was having such a hard time because my memory of high school was as it had been in the'50s, when students were mostly quiet and respectful of teachers. This was the '90s and early 2000s. Times had changed for sure! Classes were noisy, and I didn't have the organizational skills needed to be effective.

I had done great with motivated adults when I'd taught English as a second language in California. Now the difference was like night and day, and the learning curve was greater than I had anticipated. It was a little like what it must feel to walk into the higher reaches of hell.

Where was the peace and centeredness of my Holy Christ self that I knew was in me? It was there, but I was not tuned into it.

School wasn't quite like *Blackboard Jungle*, a school depicted in a 1955 movie about teachers in an interracial inner-city school. But, It was intense. I was meeting myself in these kids. What I didn't like about them I had as elements in my personality. Like attracts like, and life has a way of revealing our hang-ups by placing us with others who have the same hang-ups. The classroom became the proving ground of my internalization of the teachings I had studied. Now came the application, and at first, I was floundering.

Most of students I taught had just come from middle school and were having a difficult time adjusting to the responsibility

---

[37] "Beloved, think it not strange concerning the fiery trial which is to try you, as though some strange thing happened unto you" (1 Peter 4:12 KJV).

"Every man's work shall be made manifest: for the day shall declare it, because it shall be revealed by fire; and the fire shall try every man's work of what sort it is" (1 Corinthians 3:13 KJV).

and freedom of high school. This posed an additional hurdle for them and for me. Because initially I had a split assignment and taught in two different schools each day, I had to provide the classroom boundaries for two environments that required sometimes opposing skill sets. And I also had to travel between two schools during my lunch hour.

Finally, I got assigned to one high school. But even then, I was struggling to learn how to create guidelines like start and end times, homework check, and class rules.

Once I got that together, I had to relentlessly hold the students to these rules day in and day out. If I deviated one iota, they would find the weakest point and, through that point, would pour all of their rebellion.

I was worn out at the end of each day after what one could call a battle of the "dwellers," theirs and mine. This went on until I learned what I needed to learn.

> *Behold I have refined you but not as silver; I have*
> *tried you in the furnace of affliction.*
> —Isaiah 48:10 KJV

I took some training in effective teaching and got to observe other teachers and to receive feedback. Finally, I began to put into practice the art of teaching and how to harness all of that great student energy into something purposeful—clarity, organization, consistency, fairness, patience, and letting go of the need to always be in charge. I was learning to "lighten up" while holding to standards and to have fun and let the students have fun in the discovery and exploration of language.

These were some of the keys and tools I was putting into practice. These were the life lessons I was learning. The students were in school learning, and so was I. Earth is a schoolroom, and everywhere we are in it, we can learn something.

I often thought that what might have helped me was the discipline of judo, which is all about redirecting energy. I needed patience and mercy for myself and patience and mercy for the kids. Patience was not one of my strong suits.

The school where I worked was a very good public high school as public schools go. It enrolled about two thousand students and had one principal and four assistant principals.

My classroom was on the second floor. It had two entrances, one from the hallway that led outside and the other from a foyer that also had entrances to four other classrooms, where Spanish, French, German, and Chinese were taught. My desk was by the corner outside wall, and in the winter when I sat there to work, I was always cold. I would wrap my legs in a warm scarf, and for a while, I had a heater—until the building engineer found out. I was most always on my feet anyway.

During my fifteen years there, we had great principals and outstanding teachers who really cared about the students. Nevertheless, I had some really rebellious groups of kids. As I think about it now, I must have had karma with these particular souls, and I was there to balance it by teaching them Spanish, holding them accountable and by loving them—yes, by loving their souls, if not their individual personalities. Love balances karma.

As I said before, the very things I was encountering in the students who were testing my patience each day I was encountering

109

in myself, but I did not know it at the time. One of the most painful things for me was that I felt I had a lot to share—my interesting life experiences, traveling, and meeting new people, the spirit of adventure, and the freedom I have through knowing another language.

But the students would not allow it. They were not interested or quiet enough to be interested. I thought, *God must feel like that about me sometimes. He has so much to give—the entire universe, all of his wisdom and love—and I just want to do my thing.*

It was rare that these students gave me the opportunity to do this sharing except for the eleventh and twelfth graders, the mature ones who were about to go off to college. Otherwise, all my time was spent keeping the kids relatively quiet and involved with the lessons.

THE CELL PHONE SAGA

We had a "no-nonsense" head of security, with whom I had a very good professional relationship. There was a school-wide rule that, if you used your cell phone or tablet or even had it out during class and a teacher asked you for it, you were supposed to hand it over. You could get it back at the end of class or at the end of the day. Few paid attention to the rule. So I settled for less.

Now the rule became you could have your device out and not use it during class. Students would cheat on tests using their phones, so it was important that they kept them in their backpacks during tests. This new rule was an extended rule, and it was fair—have it out but don't use it.

Good luck with that! So I had an ongoing war over the cell phones. I wonder to this day if it was worth the hassle.

LIVING *GROUNDHOG DAY*[38]

I had one student who I had issues with about attendance and behavior. Every time she was late or disruptive, I'd call home. I really held her to account. One day, I was so frustrated with her attitude and the entire class that I told the students they could do what they wanted, I was going to my computer to do some work.

This same student looked at me and said, smiling, "Don't give up on us, Señora Frazier."

This was a surprise to me. She, and probably others, knew I really cared about them, and that made a difference to their souls. That appreciation of me was not always apparent to me. They had a momentum on "acting out" yet, deep down; they wanted me to discipline them.

So I didn't give up. I came in the next day with a new perspective, wanting to try all over again. It was like that; each day, I would try all over again. I felt like Milarepa, the Tibetan Yogi who had trials he had to repeat over and over again. It also felt like the movie *Groundhog Day*. I was teaching and re-teaching and devising rules and redevising rules, with their help, over and over again, until I got it all right. No matter what, I was going to conquer the situation and myself!

I think it took courage, but I'm not bragging. What else could I do? Give up? Never! I was in the throes of how to reach these

---

[38] *Groundhog Day* was movie about a weatherman who is caught in a time loop, reliving the same day over and over until he gets it right.

students' hearts. I was in the proving ground and was recreating myself daily, to the point where, one day, a light bulb went off in my head. Something said to me, *Stop fighting with them and yourself. Work with those who want to work and let the others be.*

So that was what I did. And you know what? As I got each student engaged, and then the next and the next, most of the class quieted down. Why did it take me so long to learn this? Was it my stubbornness? My pride? You betcha! I had the desire to control the students! When I started to let go of this desire, things calmed down.

WORKING WITH STUDENTS AND PARENTS

There was another young lady in my class who was relentlessly late and always socializing. She was cute and popular with the boys. I called home, counseled with her, and did everything I could think to get her to change her behavior. I could not reach her regardless.

And that's the way it is sometimes. God must feel like that about me too. He just can't reach me sometimes. All of us go through all of these situations—challenges, knotty problems, and puzzles. And there He is, waiting for our call, saying to us, "Look at this situation and apply my law of love. Know I love you, and I will give you the key to this knotty problem."

But we don't ask often enough or with enough persistence. God wants to be wooed. He is not an easy date. We forget that life is a great schoolroom, and the divine speaks to us through many people and directly to our hearts when we ask.

On one occasion in working with a student on changing her

behavior, I called the parent. After about four minutes, I politely hung up on her to meet my class. The truth is that I arranged to call her just five minutes before class because she had the reputation for keeping you on the phone longer than you liked. I had been warned! So rather than waiting until after school to call her, I did the caging, not so nice thing, of calling her just before class. After talking with her for four minutes or so, I explained to her that I had to go, as the bell would ring in one minute. She would not end her conversation, so I told her I would have to hang up, and I did.

She called administration, and I was called down for a meeting with her some days later. I encountered this person in the hall before I entered the conference room, and she demanded an apology. I understood right then that we were not going to have the meeting unless I apologized. So I apologized, acknowledging to myself that I had set up the situation in the first place.

Her reaction was surprising. She softened and thanked me and said that her husband had always hung up on her and that it was an issue she had been pursuing with her psychologist. She just could not let it pass with me.

At that moment, I had a lot of compassion for that parent. I was coming to understand the real meaning of, "Judge not, lest ye be judged" (Matthew 7:1–3 KJV). I realized that I perceive a person, any person, in the most limited aspect—like I mentioned before, maybe one frame in a life that has many frames or snapshots. Like the poor guy on the train whose wife had just died and he was letting his children run amok. Combine this with all the thousands of lives we all have had and the millions of snapshots of a soul over the millennia. I had to ask myself, How can I judge a person when I do not know what deeply motivates his or her behavior? The master Jesus said to judge not and for good reason.

Where had my Christ self been all this time I was teaching high school? I kept asking myself. *Where had the peace and sense of wholeness I felt in the '70s at the Summit Lighthouse gone?* I was struggling so hard to be a good teacher, to be effective and beloved by my students. Where was it?

Thinking about it now, I get it. God showed me who I was. Now I had to pull it down and make it a permanent part of myself. I had to learn, and my learning had to come from the refining fires of hard work and trial and error and lots of prayer.

It was not easy. It was very difficult, this life schooling, this proving ground. And I was taking it very seriously. I was shown what I could be in Pasadena in 1978. But now I had to fill it in, rise up to it, and become it. It was a fifteen-year initiation, and it was ongoing. I was forging my God identity.

By the end of my school career, I was successful in teaching my students. When you look at the lives of the saints, you see that they all had to go through a trial by fire. Most often for them the trial was physical—torture, scourging, crucifixion. Today, we go through these tests on the mental and emotional plane mostly and sometimes physically as disease. It is different but no less difficult and painful. It is a part of the path.

Teaching high school Spanish was a portion of what I owed to life. It was a duty. What I was learning was this: I stopped taking things personally and began to gain objectivity. My attitude toward my students changed. I accepted them for who they were and the times we lived in now. I stopped fighting with myself to try to make them as I had been as a student in the '50s.

By and by, their attitude responded positively to mine. By and by, I gained some mastery and was able to express the love and the discipline they needed in the right doses. I began fulfilling a portion of my dharma. I was developing patience, love, discipline, forgiveness, organization, intuition, and discrimination—virtues I was applying to the situations at hand.

After I retired in 2011, from time to time, I'd go to that school as a substitute, and I would see some of the same kids. They would run up to me grinning, happy to see me and give me hugs. Karma balanced?

All that I learned teaching Spanish in high school I have in my toolbox as a minister. All of it is my divine plan, ordained in the beginning when the blueprint of my life was impressed upon the white fire core of my individual I AM presence. It is the mission designed for me in particular to bring me ever closer to the reality of God within and to free me for even greater service, to teach these precious teachings to others.

Some people have a dharma that has to do with overcoming a psychological or an emotional challenge that their soul has brought with them into life for balancing. The work you have, whatever part of you it encompasses—the emotions, the mental, the physical, or all or some of them—it is the context for your overcoming. I have found that we need to do all things well, no matter where we find ourselves in life, because where we find ourselves builds a platform for the next step, the next opening, the next opportunity.

POSTSCRIPT ON TEACHING IN PUBLIC SCHOOL

As of the time of this writing I am teaching in the public school system as a substitute from time to time, and I enjoy it very much. I have a different relationship with the students now, as I am not ultimately responsible for their learning.

One day, I went to a middle school. It was a class of special education students. The teacher was very young, and you could see that she focused her attention only on the students who were working. There was a group of boys in the back who were on their cell phones watching some pretty noxious material. They would not turn their phones off even after many requests, and they were disruptive to the other students. One boy in particular just kept the disturbance going by laughing loudly and directing other students to see what he was watching.

I went over and talked with him about sitting down and doing his work (on the computer). He said he was failing the class, and it didn't matter. I tried to tell him it did matter and that, if he was failing, he could take the class again and next time, because he applied himself now, he could do better. He softened and simply said again, "I am failing."

I thought about how defeated he sounded. He had the desire to succeed; I could tell. But he was resigned to failure.

The teacher never addressed his behavior that day. I imagine she had tried to do so many times before. I knew how she felt. Silently wishing her good fortune, I closed the door on a chapter of my life and went home.

"I am failing." I thought about this boy, who had the same spark of God within him as I had. The spirit of accomplishment was there! Who would tell him? When would he realize it? Would he ever in this life? It was a sad thing really.

All this work in the classroom was preparatory to the work Kenneth and I do together as ministers.

My beloved Kenneth Frazier

I've mentioned my husband Kenneth in these memoirs but have not told you the story of how we met, which was kind of like a *Cinderella* story. I was just a reluctant Cinderella for a while. It was in June 1980, at the Washington, DC, Teaching Center on 16th Street North West, Washington, when I laid eyes on Kenneth and he on me. I had driven the two and half hours from Richmond with my two children to visit the Summit Lighthouse community for the first time. I was still married, but things were not going well.

After the service, I decided to remain in the chapel to meditate. I had my eyes closed when I sensed someone standing beside me. As I opened my eyes, I saw this impressive-looking man dressed in a white suit. I said to myself, *Who is this man dressed all in white?* Even his shoes were white—patent leather as I recall. I knew he was someone special to me, but I didn't put it together then.

He just stood there for a moment smiling at me and then introduced himself. "My name is Kenneth Frazier."

Kenneth told me some months later that he knew immediately and before approaching me that I was his wife-to-be.

At this moment, however, a future with him didn't seem possible. I was married, and although my marriage was crumbling, I had no romantic interests, and my two children were in the next room.

He asked, "What's your name?"

"Bonita Madden," I told him.

I know he observed the wedding ring on my finger. "Where do you live?"

I told him I lived in Richmond, Virginia, but that I was originally from the Bronx.

He then said, "When are you coming to California?"

I thought to myself, *What?* And then I answered, "I have no plans to come to California." Doing so was the furthest thing from my mind.

He simply smiled, his white teeth shining and said, "Well, if you ever need anything, let me know."

With that, he turned and walked away. I asked myself again, *Who is this guy?* He'd definitely made an impression.

I went to get my children. Little did I know then that, in about six months, I would be divorced and in California. And little did I know then how much Kenneth would need me and me him in the fulfillment of our work.

In less than a year, July 1980, I was in Malibu at the headquarters of the Summit Lighthouse. I will never forget how I walked out toward the lake that sunny day to visit a group of friends. Guess who was the first person to greet me? It was Kenneth Frazier, smiling as before.

He said, "Hello, Bonita. Happy to see you."

And that was the beginning of our relationship. I resisted any romantic involvement for a long time, but we did develop a friendship over a period of about a year and a half.

See, when I joined the Summit, I wanted to be a nun. I thought to myself, *I will fulfill my childhood desire.* I was finally divorced, and romance did not interest me.

But God had other plans. God knows what we need for the rounding out of our soul's experience, and I needed a good marriage with a mate who was attuned to the same things I was attuned to. I needed my partner.

I used to see Kenneth on my way to teach at Montessori, and he would just smile. And I would smile back but inwardly think, *No, no. I will not become romantically involved.*

This went on for quite a while. But I kept running into him, and he was always smiling like he knew some secret I didn't know. Have you ever met someone where, inwardly, you knew the outcome of your relationship, but you just didn't want to admit it? It was like that. I knew I was going to be Bonita Frazier.

Soon after, I learned that the messenger knew more about Kenneth and me than I knew about Kenneth and me. In the late

'70s, Mrs. Prophet, Mother, was in Crystal City, Virginia, to deliver a lecture. Both Kenneth and I were present, though we did not meet. We didn't even know each other at the time. What we pieced together many years later was our separate encounters with Mother that night.

It went like this: Following her lecture, I got on the elevator with several other people. I was thinking to myself, how it would be the end of a perfect evening to meet the messenger face-to-face. Just then, in stepped Mother with her security guard just as the door was about to close. I got a close-up look at her, and she got a close-up look at me. There were no words exchanged, just smiles.

Seconds later, I exited the elevator, and she and her security remained on the elevator as it started up again. On the next floor, Kenneth got on with Mother and her security guard and continued up with them to her suite. Earlier, he had been told Mother wanted to see him, and he was on his way up to her suite when the elevator opened, and there she was.

He spent an hour or so with her, during which she told him, "Don't get married. There is someone coming along who will be very helpful to you."

At the time, Kenneth was dating someone.

After their private conversation, Mother invited him to attend a meeting with some of her staff, which extended several hours into the morning. It was years later before we realized that both of us were at that lecture, and Mother had seen us that night on the elevator within the span of a few seconds. She saw the tie between us then and gave him her advice. God has a way of playfully arranging things for us that we are not aware of until years later.

Kenneth and I have a mission together. After many, many

121

years and incarnations of separation, we have come together again as a son and daughter of Afra to remind others like us and all light bearers of their role to fulfill the virtues of their particular ray or race, to walk the path of personal Christhood, and to ascend. We came as volunteers with the Sanat Kumara, the Ancient of Days.[39]

ASCENDED MASTER AFRA

The ascended master Afra and his sons and daughters

[39] Sanat Kumara, the Ancient of Days spoken of in Daniel 7:9, 13, and 22, long ago came to earth in her darkest hour, when no one worshipped the Christ or Mighty I AM presence. He came with 144,000 volunteers from Venus to keep the flame of life on earth until the children of God would respond to the love of God and turn once again to serve the Mighty I AM presence.

The full story of Sanat Kumara can be found in *Saint Germain on Alchemy*: Mark L. Prophet and Elizabeth C. Prophet, *Saint Germain on Alchemy: Formulas for Self-Transformation* (Gardiner, Montana: Summit University Press, 1995), glossary," The Seventh Seal).

Who are the sons and daughters of Afra? Who is Afra? Afra is an ascended master, the first to ascend from the continent of Africa. Not only was he the first from Africa to make his ascension, he was the first member of the black race to do so, and that was five hundred thousand years ago. When ascended, he asked to be called simply "a brother," or *frater* in Latin. And so "a frater" became the word Afra, from which the continent of Africa derives its name. Isn't it interesting today that we refer to the black male as a "brother?"

The story of Afra is profound and instructive. In many ways, it's the same old story of jealousy, division, and selfishness. At the time of Afra, the people in Africa had reached a crossroads. Fallen angels and dark forces had invaded the earth and were setting brother against brother, perverting their music and rituals with black magic and voodoo.

Seeing their plight, Afra took embodiment among them to help them. Many people were losing their threefold flame. The Lord said that, if they were ready to sacrifice to help their brethren and deeply care for each other, they could overcome.

Their reply was the same as Cain's. "Am I my brother's keeper?"

Afra came as the Christ to be the example and brother to all. For that, they crucified him.

This story and more about the message of Afra to sons and daughters of Afra can be found in *Afra: Brother of Light*, from the Meet the Master Series, Spiritual Teachings from an Ascended Master, published by Summit University Press in 2003.

Africa had golden ages of enlightenment and, at some time in its history, was a part of the lost continent of Lemuria. My husband,

Kenneth, remembers, out of the storehouse of his subconscious, the temples and amphitheater in Lemuria where the messenger would summon the people to hear dictations from the archangels by the sounding of a gong that reverberated throughout the city. I am sure there are others who hold in their memory distant recollections of this continent and its people. The full history of the Afra people, the golden ages in Africa, and what happened that we had to suffer slavery in the United States and other areas remains a mystery. To my knowledge, Elizabeth Clare Prophet has not written about it.[40]

It is estimated that Atlantis, the other lost continent had two golden age civilizations, one lasting from about 34,550 BC to 32,550 BC and the other from 15,000 BC to approximately 11,600 BC, when the continent sank beneath the ocean.[41]

THE MISSION OF THE BLUE AND VIOLET RACE: THE DHARMA FULL-BLOWN

The sons and daughters of Afra are those who have been working on achieving Christ consciousness for a long, long time and have

---

[40] Lemuria is referred to as the lost continent of Mu or the Motherland that, like Africa, once cradled golden age civilizations. Researchers estimate that Lemuria was destroyed approximately twelve thousand years ago by the collapse of the gas chambers that upheld the continent.

See Mark L. Prophet, Elizabeth C. Prophet, and staff of Summit University, *Sacred Adventure Series 2: Meeting the Masters* (Gardiner, Montana: Summit University Press, 2003), 17.

[41] The book *A Dweller on Two Planets* by Phylos the Tibetan describes life in Atlantis around 13,000 BC.

See W. Scott Elliot and Charles Leadbeater, *The Story of Atlantis and the Lost Lemuria* and James Churchward, *The Lost Continent of Mu*.

descended in the lineage of Sanat kumara. Originally, the hue of our skin was blue and violet. We are intended to express the attributes of the blue and violet rays—qualities of faith, power, and leadership (of the blue ray) and freedom, mercy, and justice (of the violet ray). We have come as shepherds to spiritually uplift all peoples, but especially those who identify as African or African American and other minorities from all over the world.

Through the veil of time and over the many, many centuries come and gone, we have forgotten who we are and what our great responsibility is. Kenneth, others, and myself are here to remind you of your mission and to point the direction to the great goal of life, the ascension. We are doing this through the teachings brought forth by the messenger Elizabeth Clare Prophet and the ascended masters.

Today, most people of Afra do not have a blue and violet skin tone. In some places in the world, though, where there has not been the intermingling of the races, one can see traces of the blue and the violet skin. My husband remarked that he saw this in some folks in Tallahassee, Florida.

Nowadays, what you look like does not always determine on what ray you have come to serve.[42] I have known some whites in

---

[42] The rays emanate from the color bands or spheres depicted in the causal body of the Mighty I AM presence. (See the Chart of the Mighty I AM Presence.)

The teachings of the masters reveal that, in the heaven world, one is known not by race but by the quality of one's heart and by the flame (the fire in the spiritual centers in the body) one keeps. Afra speaks of the different races as rays in the cited footnote below. He also has a lot to say about African Americans and race in the book of his dictation. You also might like to read a portion of the history of his life on the continent of Africa, what happened to him, and what he has to say about the challenges of black people in American and the world today.

Editors of the Summit Lighthouse Library, *AFRA, Brother of Light, Spiritual Teachings from an Ascended Master*, (Gardiner, Montana, Summit University Press) 2003 our community to identify strongly with Afra and some blacks that identify strongly with the yellow ray of the Chinese people. It is more an inner consideration today than a totally outer appearance.

An Interesting Experience With A Person Named Afra

I was pregnant with our son Michael. Kenneth and I were no longer living in the teaching center but with a Dr. Littlejohn and his family in Los Angeles. He was a pediatrician, and members of his family were spiritual seekers. Kenneth and I had little money and, aside from the generosity of Dr. Littlejohn, nowhere to live.

After Michael was born, Kenneth filled out an application with a local realtor named Izzy to rent a house in Canoga Park. Izzy told him that he had one house available, and there were already nine people in line to get it. "All of them are better qualified than you, but I'll take your application."

There were some friends who agreed to live with us and pick up a share of the rent until we could find jobs.

The next day, Kenneth received a call from Izzy asking him to come to his office that was just a short distance away. When he arrived, Izzy told him, "I don't know what to make of it. The owner wants you to have the house."

Kenneth was pleasantly surprised and asked what the owner's name was.

Izzy told him, "Dr. Afra."

How about that?

We lived there with several members of the Summit for a year.

For several reasons, we decided to move to another place, and we called Dr. Afra to thank him and let him know.

He asked my husband, "Where are you? Who told you to move? I didn't tell you to move."

Divine intervention or coincidence? I don't believe in coincidences.

The ascended master Afra tells us in his dictation "I Have Come to Call You Home: Call to Me" (June 27, 1999): "Therefore, be honest in your heart with your heart. Be honest in your mind with your mind. Know what you are, know what you are not. But know that always and always through your Holy Christ self and I AM presence, you have the honor of God—you have it within you, and it shall grow and grow until it becomes that fiery steel pillar."

He tells us that a universal brotherhood of man is possible to achieve. It is possible. I believe him, and I try to live by that.

At an earlier time, when Kenneth first arrived at the Ashram in 1980, Mother gave him all of the dictations and lectures that she and Mark had given in Africa during their two visits. Both Mark and Mother had gone to Ghana in the 1970s to formally introduce the continent to the new dispensation of the Teachings of the Ascended Masters. They gave landmark dictations and counsel to the groups there that are recorded and a part of a collection of teachings that we have. This material was presented to Kenneth as part of the preparation he needed for the work he was to do with the sons and daughters of Afra and other work. He was our leader, and with him, some of our members did outreach and stumped those black communities in Los Angeles and throughout the United States.

MARRIAGE

Just before we were married and during a private meeting between Mother and Kenneth, she instructed him to tell me to move with my children into the Los Angeles Teaching Center. I moved there, and we worked as directors of the center for about a year. In summer 1982, Mother asked Kenneth if he would like to get married. And at this time, I too wanted to get married. I was deeply in love and ready! She told him to bring his white suit to the summer conference in Montana.

We took our marriage vows at the end of the summer conference in the gray barn at the Royal Teton Ranch. That is the name and location of our headquarters in Montana. Rev. Peggy Keathley, a longtime staff member, officiated at our wedding. Clifford Merrill, another longtime staff member, was Kenneth's best man. A bus of Summit University[43] students on their way to the dorm stopped by the barn at the end of the ceremony to congratulate us. The cow mooed. It was truly special! We spent our honeymoon in a tent atop a seven thousand-foot mountain.

After that, Kenneth and I worked in Los Angles for about a year rearing the children from my previous marriage. Later they elected to live with their father.

Mother then said she would like us to move to Washington, DC. Kenneth worked at Howard University Hospital as its chaplain, and I taught Spanish at Amidon and Draper Elementary Schools in the District of Columbia.

---

[43] Summit University has been in the forefront of transformational learning since 1971. It pairs academic studies and professional learning with mystical and metaphysical teachings. SU also has a School of Theology and extension courses. See www.summituniversity.org.

We later moved back to Montana and lived there for five years.

TRAINING FOR LIONS-QUEST INTERNATIONAL

While living in Montana, we became trainers for Quest International, a professional development character education and drug prevention training program for teachers, school administrators, parents, and community organizations. This program was very popular in the 1980s. Kenneth and I trained thousands of teachers in elementary, middle, and high schools in character education all over the country and in Canada and Honduras. We touched lots of hearts while increasing our versatility, adaptability, and creativity.

As a part of our training, we were each under the mentorship of a senior trainer. I spent many a night preparing to present a section of a three-day workshop, only to arrive at the training and be told I had to do it all over again. So I would do it all over again, redrawing my charts and making and collecting other accessories for the lesson. I had so many do-overs during the period I was in training that I started to wonder if it was really worth it.

Not only that; when I presented my portion of the workshop, my mentor wrote down everything I said and all the things I did not say and I should have said. He included my body language and where there were inconsistencies between it and my words. It was grueling. This training went on for a period of about four months. Each time I would get to present more of the workshop.

The third and last training, my participant evaluations were high and I was accepted as a part of the international training team. My next workshop would be a "solo," with no mentor, only me. How we trainees looked forward to the "solo!"

Kenneth had a similar experience.

Yes, it was worth it! I was able to do it. I had passed this test or initiation in the professional world and learned a lot about how to motivate teachers, and about myself.

A highlight for me was training on the Navajo reservation in New Mexico. I felt I had been given the opportunity to either repay a karmic debt there or make some good karma by aiding the teachers to be more effective with their students. I also trained teachers on two Canadian reserves, while Kenneth trained on the Apache reservation. I feel God did a lot of good work through us, as we were able to influence so many educators around the country.

It was quite an experience and quite an adventure. For example, I could never predict what kind of lodging I would have when I went off to do a workshop. It depended on the school district and the amount of money that particular district had. Sometimes it would be five-star hotels with all the perks, and sometimes it would be a place you would not choose to be. We had been trained to be flexible, resilient, and skilled in working with educators of all stripes.

This work also provided us an income while living in Montana, where there was little work.

Another highlight in my life was traveling to Ghana, West Africa, in my capacity as a minister and teacher for our church's Ministerial Training Program. My husband and I also traveled to Venezuela, Mexico, Columbia, and Brazil in that capacity. These trips were great, and the people just wonderful. We were able to use a lot of the very successful training techniques we'd learned as Quest trainers.

We returned to Washington in 1996 to lead the community teaching center. Kenneth rented an office on Connecticut Avenue and opened up a psychotherapy business, and I began to teach high school Spanish—into "the fiery trial!"

TEACHING THE "TEACHINGS" WORLDWIDE

All the while, Kenneth and I still had responsibilities with our church as regional ministers. With members in our region, we developed a program on how to "Teach the Teachings" (of the ascended masters). We took this program to our membership in Colombia, Venezuela, Mexico, Canada, and Ghana, as well as throughout our region. We led sessions at the University of Pennsylvania in Philadelphia, Washington, DC, and at the Atlantic University of Miami in Broward County. These sessions brought our community together in a beautiful way. There were folks who thought they would never be able to stand up and talk to people. The practice and loving feedback the program provided gave them the skill and confidence they needed. This was very rewarding work. We loved it!

SUMMIT UNIVERSITY TEACHING ASSISTANTS

In our work today, Kenneth and I are facilitate Summit University seminars throughout the east coast of the United States. Every time we finish with one of these seminars I feel I have scaled another level of the mountain. The spiritual teachIngs are phenomenal.

We studied topics such as: Champions of Light: Conquer the Dark Side of Life, Path of the Eastern Adept and more. We are also involved in counseling, mentoring, and developing new seekers; facilitating study groups for youths and adults; and generally ministering to the communities in our region. In the spirit of ecumenism we have led silent retreats and workshops for other Christian communities as well.

MY BEST FRIEND

Kenneth is my best friend, my deepest friend, and my most loving friend, with whom I can share everything. I've had to pinch myself sometimes to register that I have such a good marriage. All of these years, we have had something special. Oh, we've had our challenges, as every couple does. When we find we have certain things we have to do independently, we give each other space and strong support. He is a Scorpio, and I am a Taurus—exact opposites. By the grace of the violet flame, we've been able to complement each other to bring out the best in both in us. That is the way it should be.

What I love so much about Kenneth is the combination of gentleness and fire (intensity). He loves God, and he loves God in people. He is always taking the time to help someone or just to talk with someone. He is the smartest man I ever met. I don't mean book smart; I mean soul smart. He reads people and situations, and he sees, by the Holy Spirit, the outplaying of events before they happen. He also has a gift of being able to communicate with the soul to soul.

Living with him, as I have for over thirty-eight years, has been wonderful, exhilarating, challenging, and fun. We talk about spiritual things all the time, especially at two and three in the morning. I count myself very fortunate to have had the good karma to share my life with someone so dear and a fellow traveler on Maitreya's mystery ship.

Recently. God gave us a gift of marriage renewal. It's like it was when we first got married, only at a new level of understanding and closeness. "'Behold, I make all things new,' saith the Lord" in Revelation 21:3–5. There is much more to that verse because in it is the Lord's promise to all of us of the new day:

> And I heard a great voice out of heaven saying, Behold, the tabernacle of God *is* with men, and he will dwell with them, and they shall be his people, and God himself shall be with them, *and be* their God.
>
> And God shall wipe away all tears from their eyes and there shall be no more death, neither sorrow nor crying, neither shall there be any more pain; for the former things are passed away.
>
> And he that sat upon the throne said, Behold, I make all things new. And he said unto me, Write: for these words are true and faithful. (Revelations 21:3–5 KJV)

Kenneth and I came together in this life to fulfill the same mission—to teach and preach the teachings of the ascended masters, to remind people of their mission given to them by God in the beginning, and to counsel those who need it.

10

To Sum Up

IF THE MESSENGER BE AN ANT, HEED HIM!

Beloved El Morya Khan, a blue ray master and founder of the Summit Lighthouse with Mark Prophet, once said, "If it, the messenger, be an ant, heed him!" The interpretation of this quote is that we can learn from everyone and everything, even the enemy, if we are open to it. Or put another way, no one is too lowly to teach us something important about ourselves.[44]

---

[44] El Morya Khan is the Chohan (chief) of the blue ray and of the Darjeeling Council. He is a great exponent of the Will of God, founder of the Summit Lighthouse, and guru to the messengers. You can read all about him and his various incarnations in *The Masters and Their Retreats*, cited many times in this manuscript.

"We have to remember what Morya says: 'If the messenger be an ant, heed him.' I'm always listening to ants. Are you? I listen to ants and every other creature that crawls or flies" (Elizabeth Clare Prophet, *Pearls of Wisdom* 51, no. 17 [July 15, 2008]).

Become a *Pearls* reader. Sign up at summitlighthouse.org.

BUDDY

One such ant in the form of a bird is my husband's African gray parrot named Buddy. His head is gray and white, and he has a red tail and a beak like an electric power drill. The African gray bonds only with one person, and Kenneth is the person. I am mostly left out of this equation.

However, I am learning a lot from Buddy. Because he is my husband's bird, he will not allow me to do certain things with him or to him. For instance, he loves to have his head scratched, but rarely does he allow me to do it, except when Kenneth is near. And sometimes he even comes at me with that power drill of a beak when I reach in his cage to give him his water. I am primarily the one who feeds him in the mornings, yet sometimes he will try to bite me when I place the food in his cage. Lately, his bites are not too hard and don't break the skin, so maybe there is hope for our relationship.

At first I was really annoyed that he would not befriend me although I fed him, cleaned his cage at times, and was the first person he saw each morning. Then I asked myself, *What is this bird teaching me?* And of course, the answer was unconditional love and that I should have no expectations of gratitude or rewards of friendship. So I started to put an end to my expectations for us to be real friends.

Then, one day when I was on the deck lying in my lounge chair soaking up some sun, Buddy, who was in his cage near me, said, "Good morning."

After a few seconds, he said it again, and I did not respond.

He then asked me, "Are you all right?"

You tell me how that bird put that thought together. I almost fell off the chair in shock.

Another time, while I was at my desk working on the computer, he did the most unexpected thing. He just climbed up on my chair and got on my shoulder and stayed there for a time.

Yet another time, as I turned off the kitchen light to go to bed he said "Good night. I love you."

I don't know if he meant it, but it sure sounded good. My heart melted. It takes time and patience to work with some fellas. It may take letting go of expectations too.

All of life is for one purpose, the ascension. And all kinds of situations present themselves to us to test our resolve, our love, and our mastery. The ascension is the "coming home for good" experience for which all of our souls thirst.

Jesus demonstrated this goal of life as an example for all of us who pursue what the ascended masters call "the Great Reunion"—the permanent reunion of our souls with the divine. This is God's will for us.

I have been consciously on this path of reunion in this life for almost forty years. Long ago, I was a wanderer in the wilderness. It wasn't until this dispensation of the coming of the messengers and the teachings of the ascended masters that I, and many others, have been given the knowledge of the path to the ascension. We have the explanation of the I AM presence chart, showing us we have an individualized Mighty I Am presence—a pictorial image of ourselves as God in potential; a Christ self that is our guide and teacher; a threefold flame in our hearts; [45] the point of contact with divinity; a causal body of light from which to draw earned virtues; and the explanation of the power of the spoken word, with which to invoke protection and transmutation. The ascended masters teach that, when we left our home in heaven to experiment in free will, God did not leave us bereft. He gave us a connection to his heart and a way home. Each one of us has been given the opportunity to explore and prove to ourselves the reality of the teachings of the ascended masters. The cosmic hierarchy has set a beautiful table full of the most sumptuous things for our souls and spirits. Will we partake of it?

We do not have to leave this world or go through the change called death to become one with the Holy Christ self. God needs

---

[45] "The Threefold flame is the flame of the Christ that is the spark of Life anchored in the secret chamber of the heart of the sons and daughters of God and the children of God. The Sacred trinity of Power, Wisdom and Love that is the manifestation of the sacred fire."

Mark L. Prophet and E. C. Prophet, *Saint Germain on Alchemy* (Montana: SU Press, 1993), glossary.

us on earth to be shining stars and to draw men and women to him. He needs us to help all humankind to learn to express His will. Is this not a wonderful plan? He desires to be God within us, to expand his beauty, power, wisdom, and love to other parts of his creation through us. This is the point of Maitreya and his mystery ship—to carry us to this most magnificent destination, which is self-transcendence and God realization.

Maitreya's ship moves on over the sea of illusion, carrying its precious cargo of light bearers who have chosen the way of freedom and eternal life. And you and I can be there in the cycle of completion if we keep on keeping on, one step at a time, passing our tests, practicing forgiveness, being kind, and giving our love and service where it is needed. The key is putting God first and allowing him to steer the course of our lives.

CLIMBING THE MOUNTAIN, LITERALLY

The phrase "one step at a time" reminds me of an experience I had at the Inner Retreat in Montana at the Royal Teton Ranch while climbing a mountain called Maitreya's Mountain. Many of our church members had climbed that mountain, and so I thought now was my turn. I set out with a small group of about seven people early one chilly Saturday morning. I did not know what I was getting into. It was quite cool, and I had on a light jacket. I was carrying about four bottles of water in my backpack and some granola bars.

Everything started out all right. About one hour into the climb, I passed an area where the forest floor leveled into a beautiful green meadow. After that, we encountered a steep path.

The mountain floor was covered with all kinds of trees—white birch, aspen, and pines—as well as rocks and moss.

I just kept moving forward and up and up and up. It was hard for me, and about an hour into the climb, everyone in my group had disappeared up the trail. And I was alone. I would climb a few yards literally and then grab a tree to hold onto, hoping it would give me some energy, some strength that I needed; and it seemed to. I would be okay for the next few yards and then hug another tree. That's how I got up the mountain—grab a tree, get some energy, and move on.

Every now and then, a solo traveler would come down the path, encouraging me. "It's not too far now. Keep on; you're almost there. You'll be all right."

I took heart from those encounters and kept moving, one foot in front of the other. But getting to the top was taking longer than I'd expected. I was glad I'd carried so much water because I needed that water, and the granola bars too.

When I got nearly to the top, almost all the way up, a strong wind came to my back and literally pushed me the rest of the way. After that moment, I fell on the ground between two large stones someone had built as an altar. Exhausted, feet and arms splayed at my sides, I gave thanks that I had made it so far. I felt a great sense of mighty victory!

Then a friend of mine came up to me with her bag filled with homeopathic remedies and gave me something for strength. I took some rest as I lay there.

This experience of climbing the mountain makes me now remember some years ago while sitting in a Summit University classroom when I had a subconscious record surface. It was the recalling of an event that had occurred a very long time ago. I was on top of a mountain with my father and brothers and resenting my father's admonishment, "Do not to go down the mountain!"

I realized in that classroom, as I was remembering the experience, that my decision had been momentous. In spite of my father's warning, I heard the revelry below and it excited my curiosity. I went down.

Having gone down, I found myself unable to climb up again no matter how hard I tried. There were others that came down also. And like me, they too were unable to climb up. We had chosen our fate. We had made our bed. And now, we had to sleep in it. My soul wept!

I am recalling this memory here to reveal my experience of God's mercy. Climbing the mountain symbolizes an opportunity all of us have to correct the errors of the past. No matter how far we may wander, you and I, God's hand, like in the famous Michelangelo painting on the ceiling of the Sistine Chapel, is extended to us. We must reach for it and want to make the climb. What a day! What a victory!

The mountain climbing experience is like the path. You don't want to give up, although it can get really tough at points. I say, keep on trucking and, like the wind and the trees that came to my rescue, you will be assisted. God wants all of us to win, and when we are sincere, his Holy Spirit will be at our backs. I did not get to the very tippy top of that mountain that afternoon. Getting where I got was the required effort for that day. There is a required effort for each day.

EPILOGUE

How I Try To Live Each Day

Muhammad Ali once said that we should live each day as if it were our last because someday we are going to be right. I try to do this, although sometimes it is a great challenge. The so-called little things are simple enough if I remember them, like a smile given to a child; a sincere compliment given to a stranger, relative, or friend, or being upbeat and positive and a pleasure to be with. How about calling someone to ask for forgiveness because, in the past, our words have hurt them or going out of our way to serve someone when we're dead tired and would rather be doing something else? From the little things to the great things, there are all kinds of ways to spread joy.

To live each day as if it were your last means prioritizing what is really important, and for me this mean starting the night before, when I plan out what I want to accomplish the next day.

Every twenty-four hours, God has a blueprint for me to fill in—something to undertake and to understand and something to master or begin to master. – a required effort. Within this blueprint is His vision of me overcoming whatever comes my way that day as karma. He doesn't personally send the karma; it comes by His law as an opportunity for redemption. And the law is that I am responsible for my own creation, good or bad, and I must balance it to reach the next rung of the ladder of enlightenment.

How do I help myself stay attuned to His will each day? I begin the day with acknowledging my Mighty I AM presence and

143

Holy Christ self. I do my spiritual ritual of decrees and prayers.[46] Sometimes when circumstances prevent it and I cannot get spiritually fortified, so to speak, I ask God to fill in the gaps. It's like calling a good friend who will fill in for you and who has your back when you really need someone to do that for you. I know God or one of His representatives, like Archangel Michael, has my back when I really need Him. I have found that God needs to be needed. He wants me to rely on Him and not on myself so much.

After the day is over and at night I review what happened. Did I accomplish what I set out to do the night before? Did I use the energy God gave me for that day responsibly? Were there any harsh words exchanged with anyone? Were my thoughts less than kind about anyone? Were there any unresolved arguments? Can I make peace now before I fall asleep? Did His plan for me that day interrupt my plan for me that day? If so, what did I learn from that interruption? Was it really an interruption or was it "the plan" from the beginning?

When it is time for bed I say my decrees and prayers and maybe meditate for a while and then ask to be taken to the retreats. Then I fall into the arms of my Mighty I AM presence, letting go of any worry or preoccupations.

It is also very valuable for me to be with a spiritual community

---

[46] The science of the spoken word is the lost art of invocation, which was practiced on Atlantis and Lemuria more than twelve thousand years ago. It is a science that has been practiced for many centuries by adepts (unascended masters) of the Far East and by Western mystics.

It outlines the uses of the voice in conjunction with the throat chakra in the giving of mantras, chants, prayers, invocations, and affirmations, as well as songs of joy and praise and fiats of light to increase the action of benign forces on earth and in the world of the individual.

See Mark L. Prophet and Elizabeth C Prophet, *The Science of the Spoken Word,* (Montana: Summit University Press, 2004), xi.

and have friends who share the same values and aspirations, as we bump auras, reinforcing and strengthening each other. These fellow travelers have the opportunity to hold the vision of my victory, and I have that same opportunity to hold it for them when sometimes it gets blurred or fades for a time.

We are all striving for the ascension—the coming-home-for-good experience at the end of a life of service to God and communities. I ascend daily by the little and big things I do in joy without rancor, without criticism, and with much love and striving.

The ascended masters are our elder brothers and sisters. They achieved enlightenment and graduated from earth's schoolroom. Their messengers were Mark L. and Elizabeth Clare Prophet, through whom they communicated to the world their teachings on the path to Christhood and Buddhahood and other mystical teachings.

I am their student. Following the path they outlined and in the imitation of Christ, I strive each day to serve from the level of my highest self and act by the power of that spirit. It is a high goal God set for me and for you. We can achieve it, by his grace.

As the days go by, my Christ consciousness envelops me more and more. I feel His presence and direction in small and large areas of my life. The love in my heart for Him and all people is intensifying and expanding. Less and less, I find myself saying and doing something I should not have said or done. I am by no means there, but I am not at the distance I once was, and in quiet times and in daily routines, I can feel the warmth and brightness of His consciousness within and around me, His love burning in my heart.

I will never be complacent. I will defend to the hilt every step won, and I will always be a learner because there is always more to learn on the path Godward.

And so, it continues.

I wish you Godspeed with all of my heart on your journey home! May you find the Pearl of Great Price!

BIBLIOGRAPHY

Barrick, Marilyn C., PhD. *Dreams Exploring: The Secrets of Your Soul.* Gardiner, Montana: Summit University Press, 2001.

————. *Sacred Psychology of Change: Life As a Voyage of Transformation.* Gardiner, Montana: Summit University Press, 2001.

Booth, A. *The Path to Your Ascension: Rediscovering Life's Ultimate Purpose.* Gardiner, Montana: SU Press.

————. *The Masters and the Path.* Recorded by Annice Booth. Gardiner, Montana: Summit University Press, 2003.

Booth, A., and Neroli Duffy. *The Practical Mystic: Life Lessons from Conversations with Mrs. Booth.* Emigrant, Montana: Darjeeling Press, 20.

Genito, Joseph with Virginia L. *Pilgrim's Victory: Journey to the Heart of God.* The Highest Mountain Press, LLC, 2016.

Kyei, Paul. *From Darkness to the Light: My Journey with the Masers.* Emigrant, Montana: Darjeeling Press, 2012.

Leadbeater, Charles. *The Inner Life.* Theosophical Publishing Company, 1978.

Lelupe, Jean-Yves. *Being Still: Reflections on an Ancient Mystical Tradition,* translated by M. S. Laird, O.S.A. New York: Paulist Press, 2003.

Prophet, Elizabeth Clare. *Becoming God: The Path of the Christian Mystic*. Gardiner, Montana: SU Press, 2010.

————. *The Buddhic Essence: The Ten Stages to Becoming a Buddha*. Gardner, Montana: SU Press

Prophet, Mark L. and C. Elizabeth. *Saint Germain on Alchemy: Formulas for Self-Transformation*. Gardiner, Montana: Summit University Press, 1993.

————. *Afra, Brother of Light: Spiritual Teachings from an Ascended Master*. Meet the Master Series. Gardiner, Montana: Summit University Press, 2003.

Prophet, Mark, recorded. *Dossier on the Ascension: Serapis Bey*. Gardiner, Montana: Summit University Press, 1978.

———— *The Chela and the Path*El Morya, Gardiner, Montana: SU Press, 1975.

————. *The Enemy Within: Encountering and Conquering the Dark Side*. Gardiner, Montana: Summit University Press, 2004.

————. *Fallen Angels Among Us: What You Need to Know*. Gardiner, Montana: Summit University Press, 2010.

————. *Fire From Heaven: The New Age of the Holy Spirit*. Gardiner, Montana, Summit Lighthouse Library, 2014.

————. *Foundations of the Path*. Gardiner, Montana: Summit University Press, 1999.

————. *The Human Aura: How to Activate and Energize Your Aura and Chakras*. Gardiner, Montana: Summit University Press, 1996.

————. *Inner Perspectives: Teachings of the Ascended Masters*. Gardiner, Montana: Summit University Press, 2001.

————. *Kabbalah: Key to Your Inner Power.*Gardiner, Montana: Summit University Press, 1997.

————. *The Masters and Their Retreats,* compiled by Annice Booth. Gardiner, Montana: SU Press, 2003.

————. *Meeting the Masters Series, Book 2.*, Gardiner, Montana: SU Press 2003

————. *The Path to Immortality*. Gardiner, Montana: Summit University Press, 2003.

————. *Paths of Light and Darkness*. Gardiner, Montana: Summit University Press, 2005.

————. *Quietly Comes the Buddha: Awakening Your Inner Buddha Nature*. Gardiner, Montana: SU Press, 1998.

————. *Reincarnation: The Missing Link in Christianity*. Montana: Summit University Press, 1997.

Prophet, Mark L., Elizabeth Clare, and the staff of SU. *The Spiritual Quest, Sacred Adventure Series*. Gardiner, Montana: SU Press, 2003.

Reichardt, Alex, and Margaret Reichardt. *All for the Love of God*. Virginia Beach, Virginia: Excelsior Publications, LLC, 2008.

Shantideva. *Guide to the Bodhisattva's Way of Life: How to Enjoy a Life of Great Meaning and Altruism*. New York: Glen Spey, Tharpa Publications, 2002.

Underhill, Evelyn. *The Essentials of Mysticism*. EU: McAllister Edition (mcallistereditions@gmail.com), 1920.

Whitfield, M. D., and Charles L. *Healing the Child Within*. Florida, Health Communications, Inc., 1987.

Yogananda, Paramahansa. *Autobiography of a Yogi*. California: Self-Realization Fellowship, Council of International Publications.

Printed in the United States
By Bookmasters